The Ultimate Lean and Green Cookbook

1000-Day Lean & Green and Fueling Hacks Recipes to Help You Manage Figure and Keep Healthy by Harnessing the Power of "Fueling Hacks Meals"

Blanche Hogan

Table of Contents

Introduction 5
   What is Lean & Green Diet ? 5
   Understanding the Food Choices 6
   Benefits of the Lean & Green Diet 7

Fueling Hacks Recipes 8
   Berry Mojito 8
   Coconut Smoothie 9
   Peppermint Mocha 10
   Shamrock Shake 11
   Chocolate Frappe 12
   Pumpkin Frappe 13
   Eggnog 14
   Hot Chocolate 15
   Pumpkin Spiced Latte 16
   Tiramisu Shake 17
   French Toast Sticks 18
   Chocolate Cake Fries 19
   Peanut Butter Bites 20
   Brownie Bites 21
   Blueberry Scones 22
   Gingersnap Cookies 23

   Peanut Butter Cookies 24
   Snicker doodles 25
   Gingerbread Biscotti 26
   Sweet Potato Muffins 27
   Peanut Butter Cups 28
   Sriracha Popcorn 29
   Mozzarella Pizza Bites 30
   Chicken Nuggets 31
   Parmesan Chicken Bites 32
   Tortilla Chips 33
   Mac & Cheese Doritos 34
   Mini Biscuit Pizza 35
   Potato Bagels 36
   Cheddar Pancakes 37

Lean & Green Recipes 38
   Broccoli Waffles 38
   Chicken & Zucchini Pancakes 39
   Green Veggies Quiche 40
   Chicken & Veggie Quiche 41
   Broccoli Frittata 42
   Kale & Mushroom Frittata 43
   Chicken & Asparagus Frittata 44

Chicken & Bell Pepper Muffins 45	Turkey with Peas 70
Eggs with Kale 46	Beef with Broccoli 71
Eggs with Spinach & Tomatoes 47	Beef with Bell Peppers 72
Turkey & Zucchini Muffins 48	Beef with Carrot & Kale 73
Tofu & Mushroom Muffins 49	Beef Chili 74
Strawberry & Asparagus Salad 50	Ground Beef with Veggies 75
Berries & Spinach Salad 51	Salmon with Cauliflower Mash 76
Chicken & Orange Salad 52	Tilapia with Asparagus 77
Steak & Tomato Salad 54	Shrimp with Zoodles 78
Salmon Salad 55	Shrimp with Spinach 79
Chicken & Kale Soup 56	Tofu with Broccoli 80
Meatballs & Spinach Soup 57	Tofu with Kale 81
Beef & Bok Choy Soup 58	Tofu with Brussels Sprout 82
Tofu & Mushroom Soup 59	Tofu with Peas 83
Chicken & Spinach Stew 60	Chicken with Bell Peppers & Onion 84
Turkey & Mushroom Stew 61	Steak with Green Beans 85
Beef & Carrot Stew 62	Steak with Mushrooms 86
Beef & Cabbage Stew 63	Scallops Salad 87
Chicken Burgers 64	Shrimp Salad 88
Turkey Burgers 65	**4 Weeks Meal Plan 89**
Beef Burgers 66	Meal Plan 5 & 1 89
Salmon Burgers 67	Meal Plan 4 & 2 & 1 93
Chicken with Zucchini 68	**Conclusion 98**
Green Chicken Curry 69	

Introduction

What is Lean & Green Diet ?

The need for a convenient meal replacement diet has seen a massive surge in recent times for its effective weight loss approach. One such famous and effective meal replacement diet is known as the Lean & Green Diet. The Lean & Green diet includes specialfood categories that include pre-packaged foods, bar, and shakes, etc. which are also known as "fuelings". It also incorporates the idea of having 'six small meals every day along with the fuelings. The Lean & Green Diet primarily focuses on an effective weight loss approach by eating small portions of food throughout the day to meet your body requirements.

Advantages and Disadvantages of the Lean & Green Diet:

Just like any other diet, the Lean & Green diet also offers certain key advantages with a few drawbacks. It is, however, important to go through them thoroughly to understand the diet more effectively. They are as follows:

Pros

- Systematic and rapid weightloss approach
- Clarity on what to eat.
- Convenience in the form of packaged foods

Cons

- Higher amount of processed food
- Restricted calories intake might result in fatigue or excessive hunger
- Increased financial burden
- Weight loss cannot be achieved once you stop following the diet

Understanding the Food Choices

There are basically two plans in the Lean & Green Diet, i.e., the 5 & 1 plan and the 4 & 2 & 1 plan. You can have low-calorie meals based on non-starchy veggies and lean proteins in addition to the fuelings. One crucial and important thing to understand is that there is no stern forbidden food category on a diet. However, various foods, especially sweets, are strongly discouraged from consumption. Healthy fats are considered good and rather are appreciated on the Lean & Green Diet.

The 5 & 1 plan is considered one of the most famous plans and is very effective in achieving strategic and rapid weight loss. You can have five fuelings and one Lean & Green low-calorie meal, i.e., preferably homemade throughout the day. The 4 & 2 & 1 plan, however, is considered best for those people who want to follow a relatively slower weight loss approach or if they want to maintain their current weight.

The Allowed Foods on the Lean & Green Diet

- Lean meats
- Fuelings
- Healthy fats
- Fresh fruits
- Low-fat dairy products
- Non-starchy and green veggies

The Restricted Foods on the Lean & Green Diet

- Alcohol
- High-calorie additives
- Sodas and sugary drinks
- Desserts that are high in calories, sugar, or fats

Benefits of the Lean & Green Diet

The Lean & Green Diet offers many health benefits that can prove to be extremely beneficial for your physical and mental health. Some of the major benefits of the diet are as follows:

1. Strategic and Rapid Weight Loss

The general requirement for daily calorie intake is around 1600 to 3000 calories per day for effective maintenance of weight. However, with the Lean & Green Diet, your calorie intake is drastically reduced to approximately 800 calories per day. It clearly indicates that the Lean & Green Diet is very effective in promoting a rapid and strategic weight loss effectively. It also enables you to shed the extra pounds in a very minimal time as compared to other weight-loss diets. The 5 & 1 plan is effectively designed to achieve rapid, systematic, and strategic weight loss. It makes it the most suitable diet for anyone who wants to lose weight extra fast for any reason.

2. Convenience Offered by Packaged Foods

The soups, shakes, and all other available meal replacement product line offered by the diet is thoroughly delivered to your doorstep to ensure your convenience as the top priority. It is not provided by any other diet, and it makes the Lean & Green Diet stand apart from its competitors. Moreover, the present ongoing Covid-19 pandemic protocols also encourage social distancing policies which can be achieved by the Lean & Green Diet as you won't have to go grocery shopping unless it's a dire emergency.

The only task you have to go out shopping is the lean & green meals which you will be preparing at home. However, the delivery options will thoroughly save you both time and energy, and the packaged products can be easily prepared within no time at all. It ensures that you have the utmost easiness around the entire idea of following the diet.

3. Promoting Clarity and Removing Doubts

It is a general perception that the hardest part of following a diet plan is to initially figure out what to eat, how to eat, and where to get all the necessary items. It takes a lot of mental energy and efforts to adjust to the entire idea of changing your eating habits out of nowhere and then having various ambiguities about the food choices. It ranges from meal to meal or even day to day in the initial days. However, the Lean & Green Diet has thoroughly figured it out for you so that you don't stress out on these pettuy things and get demotivated. The Lean & Green Diet offers its followers clear food lists that include lean & green meals. Moreover, the packaged fuelings are also provided so that you can do easy meal planning even in the early days of your plan.

Fueling Hacks Recipes

Berry Mojito

Preparation Time: 10 minutes
Servings: 2

Ingredients:

- 2 tablespoons fresh lime juice
- 6 fresh mint leaves
- 1 packet mixed berry flavor infuser
- 16 ounces seltzer water
- Ice cubes, as required

Preparation:

1. In two cocktail glasses, divide the lime juice and mint leaves.
2. With the bottom end of a spoon, gently muddle the mint leaves.
3. Now, divide the Berry Infuser and seltzer water into each glass and stir to combine.
4. Place ice cubes in each glass and serve.

Serving Suggestions: Serve with the garnishing of fresh berries.

Variation Tip: Sparkling water can be replaced with seltzer water.

Nutritional Information per Serving:

Calories: 8 | **Fat:** 0g| **Sat Fat:** 0g| **Carbohydrates:** 2.4g| **Fiber:** 1.2g| **Sugar:** 0g| **Protein:** 0.1g

Coconut Smoothie

Preparation Time: 5 minutes
Serving: 1

Ingredients:

- 6 ounces unsweetened almond milk
- 6 ounces diet ginger ale
- 2 tablespoons unsweetened coconut, shredded
- ¼ teaspoon rum extract
- ½ cup ice

Preparation:

1. In a small blender, place all ingredients and pulse until smooth.
2. Transfer the smoothie into a serving glass and serve immediately.

Serving Suggestions: Serve with the topping of unsweetened shredded coconut.

Variation Tip: Unsweetened almond milk can be replaced with unsweetened cashew milk.

Nutritional Information per Serving:

Calories: 65 | **Fat:** 5.7g | **Sat Fat:** 3.2g | **Carbohydrates:** 2.9g | **Fiber:** 1.6g |

Sugar: 0.6g | **Protein:** 1g

Peppermint Mocha

Preparation Time: 5 minutes
Serving: 1

Ingredients:

- 1 sachet Velvety Hot Chocolate
- 6 ounces freshly brewed coffee
- ¼ cup warm unsweetened almond milk
- ¼ teaspoon peppermint extract
- 1 tablespoon whipped topping
- Pinch of ground cinnamon

Preparation:

1. In a serving mug, place the hot chocolate sachet, coffee, almond milk and peppermint extract and stir until well-blended.
2. Top the hot chocolate with whipped topping and sprinkle with cinnamon.
3. Serve immediately.

Serving Suggestions: Serve with ground cinnamon topping.

Variation Tip: Make sure to use unsweetened almond milk.

Nutritional Information per Serving:

Calories: 133 | **Fat:** 2.1g | **Sat Fat:** 0.5g | **Carbohydrates:** 16.2g | **Fiber:** 4.4g | **Sugar:** 10g | **Protein:** 14.6g

Shamrock Shake

Preparation Time: 5 minutes
Serving: 1

Ingredients:

- 1 packet vanilla shake
- 6 ounces unsweetened almond milk
- ¼ teaspoon peppermint extract
- 1-2 drops green food coloring
- 1 cup ice cubes

Preparation:

1. In a small blender, place all ingredients and pulse until smooth.
2. Transfer the shake into a serving glass and serve immediately.

Serving Suggestions: Serve with mint leaves garnishing.

Variation Tip: Try to use high quality food coloring.

Nutritional Information per Serving:

Calories: 140 | **Fat:** 2.9g | **Sat Fat:** 0.2g | **Carbohydrates:** 14.5g | **Fiber:** 3.7g | **Sugar:** 9.1g | **Protein:** 14.7g

Chocolate Frappe

Preparation Time: 5 minutes
Serving: 1

Ingredients:

- 1 sachet Frosty Mint Chocolate Soft Serve Treat
- 4 ounces strong brewed coffee
- 4 ounces unsweetened almond milk
- 1 ½ tablespoons sugar-free chocolate syrup, divided
- ¼ teaspoon peppermint extract
- ½ cup ice
- 1 tablespoon whipped topping

Preparation:

1. In a blender, add the chocolate sachet, coffee, almond milk, one tablespoon of chocolate syrup, peppermint extract, ice and pulse until smooth.
2. Transfer the mixture into a glass and top with whipped topping.
3. Drizzle with remaining chocolate syrup and serve immediately.

Serving Suggestions: Serve with unsweetened cocoa powder garnishing.

Variation Tip: Make sure to use sugar-free chocolate syrup.

Nutritional Information per Serving:

Calories: 147 | **Fat:** 4.8g | **Sat Fat:** 0.6g | **Carbohydrates:** 16.4g | **Fiber:** 4.9g | **Sugar:** 7.4g | **Protein:** 11.7g

Pumpkin Frappe

Preparation Time: 5 minutes
Serving: 1

Ingredients:

- 1 sachet spiced gingerbread
- 4 ounces strong brewed coffee
- 4 ounces unsweetened almond milk
- 1/8 teaspoon pumpkin pie spice
- ½ cup ice
- 1 tablespoon whipped topping

Preparation:

1. In a blender, add the spiced gingerbread sachet, coffee, almond milk, pumpkin pie spice, ice and pulse until smooth.
2. Transfer the mixture into a glass and top with whipped topping.
3. Serve immediately.

Serving Suggestions: Serve with the sprinkling of cinnamon.

Variation Tip: You can adjust the ratio of pumpkin pie spice according to your taste.

Nutritional Information per Serving:

Calories: 138 | **Fat:** 4.8g | **Sat Fat:** 0.6g | **Carbohydrates:** 15.4g | **Fiber:** 4.5g | **Sugar:** 5g | **Protein:** 11.7g

Eggnog

Preparation Time: 5 minutes
Serving: 1

Ingredients:

- 1 sachet vanilla shake
- 8 ounces unsweetened almond milk
- 1 egg (yolk and white separated)
- ¼ teaspoon rum extract
- Pinch of ground nutmeg

Preparation:

1. In a blender, add the vanilla shake sachet, almond milk, egg yolk and pulse until smooth.
2. In the bowl of a stand mixer, place egg white and beat on medium speed until stiff peaks form.
3. Place the whipped egg whites into a serving glass and top with shake mixture.
4. Stir the mixture and sprinkle with nutmeg.
5. Serve immediately.

Serving Suggestions: Serve with the topping of whipped topping.

Variation Tip: You can skip rum extract.

Nutritional Information per Serving:

Calories: 103 | **Fat:** 8.7g | **Sat Fat:** 1.7g | **Carbohydrates:** 15.6g | **Fiber:** 5g | **Sugar:** 7.4g | **Protein:** 21.5g

Hot Chocolate

Preparation Time: 10 minutes
Cooking Time: 2 minutes
Serving: 1

Ingredients:

- 1 sachet velvety hot chocolate
- ½ teaspoon ground cinnamon
- Pinch of cayenne pepper
- 6 ounces unsweetened almond milk
- 1 tablespoon whipped cream

Preparation:

1. In a serving mug, place all the ingredients except for whipped cream and beat until well-blended.
2. Microwave on high for about two minutes.
3. Top with whipped cream and serve.

Serving Suggestions: Serve with unsweetened chocolate chips on the top.

Variation Tip: Ground cinnamon can be replaced with ground nutmeg.

Nutritional Information per Serving:

Calories: 185 | **Fat:** 8.1g | **Sat Fat:** 3.1g | **Carbohydrates:** 15.9g | **Fiber:** 5.4g | **Sugar:** 9.1g | **Protein:** 14.1g

Pumpkin Spiced Latte

Preparation Time: 5 minutes
Cooking Time: 1 minute
Serving: 1

Ingredients:

- ½ cup unsweetened cashew milk
- 2 tablespoons pumpkin puree
- ½ cup strong brewed coffee
- 1 sachet spiced gingerbread

Preparation:

1. In a microwave-safe mug, place cashew milk, pumpkin puree and microwave for one minute.
2. Remove from microwave and immediately stir in coffee and gingerbread sachet until smooth.
3. Serve immediately.

Serving Suggestions: Serve with ground nutmeg garnishing.

Variation Tip: For best result, use sugar-free pumpkin puree.

Nutritional Information per Serving:

Calories: 134 | **Fat:** 3.5g | **Sat Fat:** 20g | **Carbohydrates:** 17g | **Fiber:** 5g | **Sugar:** 6g | **Protein:** 11.4g

Tiramisu Shake

Preparation Time: 5 minutes
Serving: 1

Ingredients:

- 1 packet cappuccino mix
- 1 tablespoon sugar-free chocolate syrup
- ½ cup water
- ½ cup ice, crushed

Preparation:

1. In a small blender, add all the ingredients and pulse until smooth and creamy.
2. Transfer the shake into a serving glass and serve immediately.

Serving Suggestions: Serve with cacao powder sprinkling.

Variation Tip: Sugar-free chocolate syrup can be replaced with sugar-free caramel syrup.

Nutritional Information per Serving:

Calories: 107 | **Fat:** 0g | **Sat Fat:** 0g | **Carbohydrates:** 15g | **Fiber:** 4.5g | **Sugar:** 8g | **Protein:** 14g

French Toast Sticks

Preparation Time: 15 minutes
Cooking Time: 4 minutes
Servings: 3

Ingredients:

- 2 sachets Cinnamon Crunchy Oat Cereal
- 6 tablespoons egg liquid substitute
- 2 tablespoons low-fat cream cheese, softened
- Non-stick cooking spray

Preparation:

1. In a food processor, add the cereal sachets and pulse until fine breadcrumbs like consistency is achieved.
2. Add the egg liquid substitute and cream cheese and pulse until a dough forms.
3. Divide the dough into six portions and shape each into a breadstick.
4. Heat a lightly greased wok over medium-high heat and cook the French toast sticks for about two minutes per side or until golden brown.
5. Serve warm.

Serving Suggestions: Serve with maple syrup on the top.

Variation Tip: Olive oil cooking spray will be a best choice in this recipe.

Nutritional Information per Serving:

Calories: 140 | **Fat:** 3.3g | **Sat Fat:** 1.5g | **Carbohydrates:** 15.4g | **Fiber:** 4g | **Sugar:** 2.2g | **Protein:** 15.2g

Chocolate Cake Fries

Preparation Time: 10 minutes
Cooking Time: 4 minutes
Servings: 2

Ingredients:

- 2 sachets Golden Chocolate Chip Pancakes
- ¼ cup liquid egg substitute
- 2 teaspoons vegetable oil

Preparation:

1. In a bowl, add pancake sachets and egg substitute and mix until well-combined.
2. Place the mixture into a resealable plastic bag.
3. Cut off a small hole on tip of the bag.
4. In a wok, heat oil over medium heat.
5. In the wok, pipe mixture in long, straight lines and cook for about two minutes per side.
6. Serve warm.

Serving Suggestions: Serve with sugar-free chocolate syrup on the top.

Variation Tip: Don't overcook the fries.

Nutritional Information per Serving:

Calories: 167 | **Fat:** 6g | **Sat Fat:** 1.9g | **Carbohydrates:** 16.2g | **Fiber:** 4g | **Sugar:** 6.2g | **Protein:** 14.8g

Peanut Butter Bites

Preparation Time: 10 minutes
Cooking Time: 1 minute
Serving: 1

Ingredients:

- 2 tablespoons peanut butter powder
- 1 tablespoon water
- 1 sachet Creamy Double Peanut Butter Crisp Bar

Preparation:

1. In a bowl, add the peanut butter powder and water and mix until a smooth paste is formed.
2. In a microwave-safe plate, place the crisp bar and microwave for about 15 seconds or until soft.
3. Add the warm bar pieces into the bowl of water mixture and mix until a dough forms.
4. Make small four equal-sized balls from the dough and arrange onto a parchment paper-lined plate.
5. Refrigerate until set before serving.

Serving Suggestions: Serve with unsweetened shredded coconut on the top.

Variation Tip: Strictly follow the ratio of ingredients.

Nutritional Information per Serving:

Calories: 190 | **Fat:** 5.5g | **Sat Fat:** 1.5g | **Carbohydrates:** 17g | **Fiber:** 6g | **Sugar:** 9g | **Protein:** 17g

Brownie Bites

Preparation Time: 10 minutes
Servings: 6

Ingredients:

- 3 tablespoons peanut butter powder
- 1 cup plus 3 tablespoons water, divided
- 6 sachets double chocolate brownie mix

Preparation:

1. In a small bowl, add the peanut butter powder and three tablespoons of water and mix until well combined.
2. In another bowl, add double chocolate brownie sachets and remaining water, and mix until well-combined.
3. In the bottom of six silicon molds, place the peanut butter powder mixture evenly and top with brownie mixture.
4. Freeze the molds until set completely.
5. Remove from the freezer and set aside for about 30-40 minutes before serving.

Serving Suggestions: Serve with sugar-free chocolate syrup on the top.

Variation Tip: Use best quality peanut butter powder.

Nutritional Information per Serving:

Calories: 137 | **Fat:** 3g | **Sat Fat:** 1.2g | **Carbohydrates:** 16.5g | **Fiber:** 5.1g | **Sugar:** 8g | **Protein:** 15g

Blueberry Scones

Preparation Time: 15 minutes
Cooking Time: 20 minutes
Servings: 6

Ingredients:

- 4 sachets Blueberry Almond Hot Cereal
- ¼ cup ground flaxseed
- 1-2 packets zero-calorie sugar substitute
- ½ teaspoon baking powder
- 3 tablespoons frozen unsalted butter, cut into ½-inch pieces
- 3 tablespoons low-fat plain Greek yogurt
- ¼ teaspoon almond extract
- ¼ teaspoon ground cinnamon

Preparation:

1. Preheat your oven to 400° F.
2. Line a baking sheet with parchment paper.
3. In a food processor, add the hot cereal sachet, flaxseed, sugar substitute and baking powder, and pulse until well blended.
4. Add the butter and pulse until a coarse meal-like mixture is formed.
5. Add the yogurt and almond extract and pulse until just blended.
6. Place the dough onto the prepared baking sheet and shape into a six-inch circle.
7. Sprinkle the top of the dough circle with cinnamon.
8. Bake for approximately 15-20 minutes or until top becomes golden brown.
9. Remove the baking sheet from oven and set aside to cool.
10. Cut the dough circle into six wedges and serve.

Serving Suggestions: Serve with powdered sugar substitute sprinkling.

Variation Tip: Almond extract can be replaced with vanilla extract.

Nutritional Information per Serving:

Calories: 155 | **Fat:** 8.6g | **Sat Fat:** 3.9g | **Carbohydrates:** 12.2g | **Fiber:** 3.9g | **Sugar:** 1.9g | **Protein:** 8.7g

Gingersnap Cookies

Preparation Time: 10 minutes
Cooking Time: 20 minutes
Serving: 1

Ingredients:

- 1 sachet spiced gingerbread
- 2 tablespoons cold water
- Olive oil cooking spray
- 2 tablespoons low-fat whipped cream cheese spread
- 1/8 teaspoon vanilla extract
- 3-5 drops liquid stevia

Preparation:

1. Preheat your oven to 350° F.
2. Lightly grease a cookie sheet.
3. In a bowl, add spiced gingerbread sachet and beat until smooth.
4. With a small spoon, place about three cookies onto the prepared cookie sheet in a single layer.
5. Bake for approximately 18-20 minutes or until golden brown.
6. Remove from the oven and place the cookie sheet onto a wire rack to cool for about five minutes.
7. Now, invert the cookies onto the wire rack to cool before serving.
8. Meanwhile, in a small bowl, place cream cheese, vanilla extract and stevia and beat until smooth.
9. Spread frosting over cookies and serve.

Serving Suggestions: Enjoy with a cup of warm non-dairy milk.

Variation Tip: Vanilla extract can be replaced with almond extract.

Nutritional Information per Serving:

Calories: 142 | **Fat:** 2.5g | **Sat Fat:** 0g | **Carbohydrates:** 16.1g | **Fiber:** 4g | **Sugar:** 6.1g | **Protein:** 15g

Peanut Butter Cookies

Preparation Time: 10 minutes
Cooking Time: 12 minutes
Servings: 4

Ingredients:

- 4 sachets Silky Peanut Butter Shake
- ¼ teaspoon baking powder
- ¼ cup unsweetened almond milk
- 1 tablespoon margarine, softened
- ¼ teaspoon vanilla extract
- 1/8 teaspoon sea salt

Preparation:

1. Preheat your oven to 350° F. Line a cookie sheet with parchment paper.
2. In a bowl, add the peanut butter shake and baking powder, and mix well.
3. Add the almond milk, margarine and vanilla extract and mix until well blended.
4. With a spoon, place eight cookies onto the prepared cookie sheet in a single layer and with a fork, press each ball slightly.
5. Sprinkle salt on each cookie and bake for approximately 10-12 minutes.
6. Remove from the oven and place the cookie sheet onto a wire rack to cool for about five minutes.
7. Now, invert the cookies onto the wire rack to cool before serving.

Serving Suggestions: Serve with powdered sugar substitute on the top.

Variation Tip: Use unsalted margarine.

Nutritional Information per Serving:

Calories: 139 | **Fat:** 5.6g | **Sat Fat:** 0.5g | **Carbohydrates:** 15.3g | **Fiber:** 4.1g | **Sugar:** 13g | **Protein:** 0.8g

Snicker doodles

Preparation Time: 10 minutes
Cooking Time: 8 minutes
Servings: 2

Ingredients:

- 2 packets French Vanilla Shake
- 1 packet Splenda with Fiber
- 1 teaspoon baking powder
- ¼ teaspoon ground cinnamon
- 1 teaspoon vanilla extract
- ¼ cup water

Preparation:

1. Preheat your oven to 350° F. Line a cookie sheet with parchment paper.
2. In a bowl, add the vanilla shake packet, Splenda, baking powder and cinnamon, and mix well.
3. Add the vanilla extract and mix well.
4. Slowly, add the water and mix until a paste is formed.
5. With a spoon, place four cookies onto the prepared cookie sheet in a single layer and with your fingers, press each ball slightly.
6. Bake for approximately eight minutes.
7. Remove from oven and place the cookie sheet onto a wire rack to cool for about five minutes.
8. Now, invert the cookies onto the wire rack to cool before serving.

Serving Suggestions: Serve with melted margarine drizzling.

Variation Tip: Splenda with fiber can be replaced with Erythritol.

Nutritional Information per Serving:

Calories: 129 | **Fat:** 0.5g | **Sat Fat:** 0g | **Carbohydrates:** 16g | **Fiber:** 4.2g | **Sugar:** 11.3g | **Protein:** 14g

Gingerbread Biscotti

Preparation Time: 15 minutes
Cooking Time: 45 minutes
Servings: 2

Ingredients:

- 1 sachet spiced gingerbread
- ¼ teaspoon baking powder
- 2 tablespoons sugar-free maple syrup
- 2 egg whites

Preparation:

1. Preheat your oven to 350° F. Line a baking sheet with parchment paper.
2. In a bowl, mix together the gingerbread sachet and baking powder.
3. In the bowl, add the maple syrup and egg whites and mix until well-blended.
4. With lightly greased hands, place the dough onto the prepared baking sheet.
5. With your hands, shape the dough into an 8-inch-long log.
6. Bake for approximately 25-30 minutes or until the top is firm.
7. Remove the baking sheet from oven and set aside to cool for about 5-10 minutes.
8. Cut the log into 8 (1-inch thick) slices.
9. Arrange the biscotti slices onto the baking sheet in a single layer, cut side down.
10. Now, set the temperature of the oven to 325° F and Bake for approximately 15 minutes.
11. Remove the baking sheet from oven and place the baking sheet onto a wire rack to cool for about five minutes.
12. Now, invert the biscotti sticks onto the wire rack to cool before serving.

Serving Suggestions: Serve with sugar-free berry jam.

Variation Tip: Make sure to use sugar-free maple syrup.

Nutritional Information per Serving:

Calories: 83 | **Fat:** 1.4g | **Sat Fat:** 0g | **Carbohydrates:** 10.3g | **Fiber:** 0g | **Sugar:** 2.7g | **Protein:** 9.1g

Sweet Potato Muffins

Preparation Time: 10 minutes
Cooking Time: 15 minutes
Serving: 1

Ingredients:

- 1 sachet Honey Sweet Potatoes
- ½ cup water
- 2 tablespoons egg beaters
- ¼ teaspoon baking powder
- Pinch of ground cinnamon

Preparation:

1. Preheat your oven to 350° F.
2. Lightly grease two cups of a standard-sized muffin tin.
3. In a bowl, add all ingredient except for cinnamon and mix until well-combined.
4. Place the mixture into the prepared muffin cups evenly and sprinkle with cinnamon.
5. Bake for approximately 15 minutes or until a toothpick inserted in the center comes out clean.
6. Remove the muffin tin from oven and place onto a wire rack to cool for about ten minutes.
7. Carefully invert the muffins onto the wire rack to cool completely before serving.

Serving Suggestions: Serve with chopped walnuts on the top.

Variation Tip: You can increase the ground cinnamon ratio according to your taste.

Nutritional Information per Serving:

Calories: 119 | **Fat:** 0g | **Sat Fat:** 0g | **Carbohydrates:** 16g | **Fiber:** 4.2g | **Sugar:** 3.2g | **Protein:** 14.9g

Peanut Butter Cups

Preparation Time: 15 minutes
Servings: 4

Ingredients:

- 2 sachets Decadent Double Chocolate Brownie
- 9-10 tablespoons unsweetened almond milk, divided
- ¼ cup powdered peanut butter

Preparation:

1. In a small bowl, add the brownie sachet and six tablespoons of almond milk and mix well.
2. In another bowl, add the remaining milk and peanut butter powder and mix well
3. In two different pipping bags, place the brownie mixture and peanut butter powder mixture respectively.
4. In the bottom of 20 silicone baking molds, place about half of the brownie mixture.
5. Top each mold with a little peanut butter powder mixture.
6. Place the remaining brownie mixture on top evenly.
7. Freeze for at least two hours before serving.

Serving Suggestions: Serve with chopped peanuts on the top.

Variation Tip: Almond milk can be replaced with cashew milk.

Nutritional Information per Serving:

Calories: 129 | **Fat:** 3.2g | **Sat Fat:** 1g | **Carbohydrates:** 15.6g | **Fiber:** 4.8g | **Sugar:** 11.3g | **Protein:** 3.7g

Sriracha Popcorn

Preparation Time: 5 minutes
Serving: 1

Ingredients:

- 1 teaspoon unsalted butter, melted
- 1 teaspoon Sriracha
- Pinch of stevia powder
- 1 sachet Sharp Cheddar & Sour Cream Popcorn

Preparation:

1. In a zip lock bag, place all ingredients.
2. Seal the bag and shake to coat well.
3. Serve immediately.

Serving Suggestions: Serve with the drizzling of extra butter.

Variation Tip: Stevia powder can be replaced with maple syrup.

Nutritional Information per Serving:

Calories: 109 | **Fat:** 7.6g | **Sat Fat:** 2.4g | **Carbohydrates:** 7g | **Fiber:** 1g | **Sugar:** 0g | **Protein:** 1g

Mozzarella Pizza Bites

Preparation Time: 15 minutes
Cooking Time: 12 minutes
Servings: 4

Ingredients:

- 4 packets Buttermilk Cheddar Herb Biscuit
- Olive oil cooking spray
- 3 plum tomatoes, sliced thinly
- 1 cup fresh basil leaves, julienned
- ½ cup unsweetened almond milk
- 2 teaspoons olive oil
- 4 ounces part-skim mozzarella cheese, cut into small pieces
- 2 tablespoons balsamic vinegar

Preparation:

1. Preheat your oven to 450° F.
2. Lightly grease a 12 cups muffin tin.
3. In a bowl, add the biscuit sachet, almond milk and oil and mix until well-combined.
4. Place the biscuit mixture into the prepared muffin cups evenly.
5. Place a mozzarella piece over biscuit mixture, followed by the one tomato slice and basil pieces.
6. Bake for approximately 10-12 minutes or until cheese is bubbly.
7. Remove from the oven and set aside to cool slightly.
8. Serve warm with the drizzling of vinegar.

Serving Suggestions: Serve with fresh herbs garnishing.

Variation Tip: Balsamic vinegar can be replaced with fresh lime juice.

Nutritional Information per Serving:

Calories: 230 | **Fat:** 10.5g | **Sat Fat:** 6.3g | **Carbohydrates:** 17.8g | **Fiber:** 5.3g | **Sugar:** 4.8g | **Protein:** 19g

Chicken Nuggets

Preparation Time: 10 minutes
Cooking Time: 20 minutes
Servings: 4

Ingredients:

- 1 egg
- 12 ounces boneless, skinless chicken breast, cubed
- Olive oil cooking spray
- 2 sachets Honey Mustard & Onion Sticks, crushed finely

Preparation:

1. Preheat your oven to 400° F.
2. Line a rimmed baking sheet with a lightly greased piece of foil.
3. In a shallow bowl, crack the egg and beat well.
4. In another shallow bowl, place the crushed onion sticks.
5. Dip the chicken cubes in beaten egg and then coat with crushed sticks.
6. Arrange the coated chicken cubes onto the prepared baking sheet in a single layer and spray with cooking spray.
7. Bake for approximately 18-20 minutes, flipping once halfway through.
8. Serve warm.

Serving Suggestions: Enjoy with your favorite dipping sauce.

Variation Tip: cut the chicken breast into uniform-sized cubes.

Nutritional Information per Serving:

Calories: 163 | **Fat:** 3.9g | **Sat Fat:** 0.3g | **Carbohydrates:** 6.6g | **Fiber:** 1.3g | **Sugar:** 1.1g | **Protein:** 24.9g

Parmesan Chicken Bites

Preparation Time: 15 minutes
Cooking Time: 30 minutes
Servings: 2

Ingredients:

- 2 packets Parmesan Cheese Puffs, crushed finely
- 2 ounces boneless, skinless chicken breast, cubed
- 2 tablespoons low-fat Parmesan cheese, grated
- 2 tablespoons hot sauce

Preparation:

1. Preheat your oven to 350° F.
2. Line a baking sheet with parchment paper.
3. In a plastic ziploc bag, place the crushed parmesan puffs and Parmesan cheese and mix well.
4. In a bowl, add chicken cubes and hot sauce and toss to coat well.
5. Place the coated chicken cubes in bag with parmesan mixture.
6. Seal the bag and shake to coat well.
7. Arrange the coated chicken cubes onto the prepared baking sheet in a single layer.
8. Bake for approximately 25-30 minutes.
9. Serve warm.

Serving Suggestions: Enjoy with sugar-free ketchup.

Variation Tip: Parmesan cheese can be replaced with Asiago cheese.

Nutritional Information per Serving:

Calories: 157 | **Fat:** 4.8g | **Sat Fat:** 1.2g | **Carbohydrates:** 14.3g | **Fiber:** 4g | **Sugar:** 1.2g | **Protein:** 18.1g

Tortilla Chips

Preparation Time: 10 minutes
Cooking Time: 25 minutes
Servings: 2

Ingredients:

- 2 sachets Hearty Red Bean & Vegetable Chili
- ¼ cup water

Preparation:

1. Preheat your oven to 350° F.
2. Line a rimmed baking sheet with a lightly greased parchment paper.
3. In a food processor, add the vegetable chili sachet and pulse until finely powdered.
4. Transfer the vegetable chili powder into a bowl with water and beat until smooth.
5. Arrange the dough onto the prepared baking sheet and with your hands, smooth the top surface.
6. With a knife, cut the dough into chips-size pieces.
7. Bake for approximately ten minutes.
8. Carefully flip the dough pieces and bake for approximately 10-15 minutes.
9. Remove the baking sheet of chips from the oven and set aside to cool before serving.

Serving Suggestions: Serve with fresh salsa.

Variation Tip: You can also score the chips with a pizza cutter.

Nutritional Information per Serving:

Calories: 110 | **Fat:** 1g | **Sat Fat:** 0g | **Carbohydrates:** 15g | **Fiber:** 4g | **Sugar:** 4g | **Protein:** 12g

Mac & Cheese Doritos

Preparation Time: 15 minutes
Cooking Time: 15 minutes
Serving: 1

Ingredients:

- 1 packet macaroni & cheese
- ¼ teaspoon garlic salt
- ¼ teaspoon red pepper flakes, crushed
- 2 tablespoons water
- Pinch of red chili powder
- Non-stick cooking spray

Preparation:

1. Preheat your oven to 350° F.
2. In a food processor, add mac & cheese packet, garlic salt and red pepper flakes, and pulse until finely powdered.
3. Transfer into a bowl with water and stir to combine.
4. Set aside for about 2 minutes.
5. Place the dough between two greased pieces of parchment and with your hands, spread into a thin circle.
6. Carefully peel off the top layer of parchment.
7. Arrange the dough onto a baking sheet alongside the parchment paper.
8. Sprinkle the dough with chili powder.
9. Bake for approximately ten minutes.
10. Remove from the oven and with a pizza cutter, cut into chip-size pieces.
11. Flip the chips and bake for approximately 3-5 minutes.
12. Remove from the oven and set aside to cool completely before serving.

Serving Suggestions: Serve with tomato sauce.

Variation Tip: You can use simple salt instead of garlic salt.

Nutritional Information per Serving:

Calories: 115 | **Fat:** 1.7g | **Sat Fat:** 0g | **Carbohydrates:** 15.9g | **Fiber:** 4.3g | **Sugar:** 1.2g | **Protein:** 11.2g

Mini Biscuit Pizza

Preparation Time: 10 minutes
Cooking Time: 14 minutes
Servings: 1

Ingredients:

- 1 sachet Buttermilk Cheddar and Herb Biscuit
- 2 tablespoons water
- 1 tablespoon tomato sauce
- 1 tablespoon low-fat cheddar cheese, shredded

Preparation:

1. Preheat your oven to 350° F.
2. In a small bowl, add the biscuit and water and mix well.
3. Place the biscuit mixture onto a parchment paper and with a spoon, spread into a thin circle.
4. Bake for approximately ten minutes.
5. Remove from the oven and spread the tomato sauce over the biscuit circle.
6. Sprinkle with cheddar cheese.
7. Bake for approximately 2-4 minutes or until cheese is melted.
8. Remove from the oven and set aside for about 3-5 minutes.
9. Serve warm.

Serving Suggestions: Serve with olives on the top.

Variation Tip: Use sugar-free tomato sauce.

Nutritional Information per Serving:

Calories: 142 | **Fat:** 5.4g | **Sat Fat:** 2.3g | **Carbohydrates:** 13.9g | **Fiber:** 4.2g | **Sugar:** 2.7g | **Protein:** 13g

Potato Bagels

Preparation Time: 10 minutes
Cooking Time: 12 minutes
Serving: 1

Ingredients:

- 2 egg whites
- 1 sachet mashed potatoes
- 1 teaspoon baking powder

Preparation:

1. Preheat your oven to 350° F.
2. Lightly grease one hole of a donut pan.
3. In a bowl, add the egg whites and beat until foamy.
4. Add the baking powder and mashed potatoes and beat until well-blended.
5. Place the mixture into the prepared donut hole.
6. Bake for approximately 10-12 minutes or until done.
7. Serve warm.

Serving Suggestions: Serve with unsalted butter topping.

Variation Tip: Use a wire whisk to whip the egg whites.

Nutritional Information per Serving:

Calories: 149 | **Fat:** 0.6g | **Sat Fat:** 0g | **Carbohydrates:** 16.8g | **Fiber:** 4.1g | **Sugar:** 2.5g | **Protein:** 18.2g

Cheddar Pancakes

Preparation Time: 10 minutes
Cooking Time: 12 minutes
Servings: 2

Ingredients:

- 1 garlic mashed potatoes
- ¼ cup low-fat cheddar cheese, shredded
- ¼ teaspoon baking powder
- ½ cup water
- 2 tablespoons low-fat sour cream

Preparation:

1. In a bowl, add all the ingredients except for sour cream and mix until well-blended.
2. Set the bowl of mixture aside for about five minutes.
3. Heat a lightly greased cast-iron wok over medium heat.
4. Place half of the mixture and with the back of a spoon, spread the mixture into a circle.
5. Cook for about 2-3 minutes per side or until golden brown.
6. Repeat with the remaining mixture.
7. Serve warm with the topping of sour cream.

Serving Suggestions: Serve with scallion greens garnishing.

Variation Tip: Use low-fat sour cream.

Nutritional Information per Serving:

Calories: 138 | **Fat:** 7.4g | **Sat Fat:** 2.1g | **Carbohydrates:** 8.5g | **Fiber:** 2g | **Sugar:** 1.1g | **Protein:** 9.4g

Lean & Green Recipes

Broccoli Waffles

Preparation Time: 10 minutes
Cooking Time: 8 minutes
Servings: 2

Ingredients:

- ¾ cup broccoli, chopped finely
- ½ cup low-fat Cheddar cheese, shredded
- 2 eggs
- 1 teaspoon garlic powder
- 1 teaspoon dried onion, minced
- Pinch of red pepper flakes, crushed
- Salt and ground black pepper, as required

Preparation:

1. Preheat a waffle iron and then grease it.
2. In a medium bowl, place all ingredients and mix until well-combined.
3. Place ½ of the mixture into preheated waffle iron and cook for about 3-4 minutes or until golden brown.
4. Repeat with the remaining mixture.
5. Serve warm.

Serving Suggestions: Serve with low-fat sour cream topping.

Variation Tip: Adjust the ratio of spices according to your taste.

Nutritional Information per Serving:

Calories: 97 | **Fat:** 7g | **Sat Fat:** 3.7g | **Carbohydrates:** 2g | **Fiber:** 0.5g | **Sugar:** 0.7g | **Protein:** 6.9g

Chicken & Zucchini Pancakes

Preparation Time: 15 minutes
Cooking Time: 32 minutes
Servings: 4

Ingredients:

- 4 cups zucchinis, shredded
- Salt, as required
- ¼ cup cooked chicken, shredded
- ¼ cup scallion, chopped finely
- 1 egg, beaten
- ¼ cup coconut flour
- Salt and ground black pepper, as required
- 1 tablespoon extra-virgin olive oil

Preparation:

1. In a colander, place the zucchini and sprinkle with salt.
2. Set aside for about 8-10 minutes.
3. Squeeze the zucchinis well and transfer into a bowl.
4. In the bowl of zucchini, add the remaining ingredients and mix until well-combined.
5. In a large non-stick wok, heat the oil over medium heat.
6. Add ¼ cup of zucchini mixture into the preheated wok and spread in an even layer.
7. Cook for about 3-4 minutes per side.
8. Repeat with the remaining mixture.
9. Serve warm.

Serving Suggestions: Serve alongside the plain yogurt.

Variation Tip: Scallion can be replaced with fresh chives.

Nutritional Information per Serving:

Calories: 84 | **Fat:** 5.2g | **Sat Fat:** 1.1g | **Carbohydrates:** 4.8g | **Fiber:** 1.7g | **Sugar:** 2.2g | **Protein:** 5.5g

Green Veggies Quiche

Preparation Time: 15 minutes
Cooking Time: 20 minutes
Servings: 4

Ingredients:

- 6 eggs
- ½ cup unsweetened almond milk
- Salt and ground black pepper, as required
- 2 cups fresh baby spinach, chopped
- ½ cup green bell pepper, seeded and chopped
- 1 scallion, chopped
- ¼ cup fresh cilantro, chopped
- 1 tablespoon fresh chives, minced
- 3 tablespoons part-skim mozzarella cheese, grated

Preparation:

1. Preheat your oven to 400° F.
2. Lightly grease a pie dish.
3. In a large bowl, add the eggs, almond milk, salt and black pepper and beat until well-combined. Set aside.
4. In another bowl, add the vegetables and herbs and mix well.
5. In the bottom of prepared pie dish, place the veggie mixture evenly and top with the egg mixture.
6. Bake for approximately 20 minutes or until a wooden skewer inserted in the center comes out clean.
7. Remove from the oven and immediately sprinkle with the Parmesan cheese.
8. Set aside for about five minutes before slicing.
9. Cut into desired sized wedges and serve.

Serving Suggestions: Serve with fresh greens.

Variation Tip: Baby spinach can be replaced with baby kale.

Nutritional Information per Serving:

Calories: 169 | **Fat:** 10.9g | **Sat Fat:** 4.4g | **Carbohydrates:** 3.5g | **Fiber:** 0.8g | **Sugar:** 1.4g | **Protein:** 15.1g

Chicken & Veggie Quiche

Preparation Time: 15 minutes
Cooking Time: 25 minutes
Servings: 4

Ingredients:

- 6 eggs
- ½ cup unsweetened almond milk
- Salt and ground black pepper, as required
- 1 cup cooked chicken, chopped
- ½ cup fresh baby spinach, chopped
- ½ cup fresh baby kale, chopped
- ¼ cup fresh mushrooms, sliced
- ¼ cup green bell pepper, seeded and chopped
- 1 scallion, chopped
- ¼ cup fresh cilantro, chopped
- 1 tablespoon fresh chives, minced

Preparation:

1. Preheat the oven to 400° F.
2. Lightly grease a pie dish.
3. In a large bowl, add the eggs, almond milk, salt and black pepper and beat well. Set aside.
4. In another bowl, add the chicken, vegetables, scallion and herbs and mix well.
5. Place the chicken mixture in the bottom of the prepared pie dish.
6. Place the egg mixture over chicken mixture evenly.
7. Bake for approximately 20 minutes or until a toothpick inserted in the center comes out clean.
8. Remove from the oven and set aside to cool for about 5-10 minutes before slicing.
9. Cut into desired size wedges and serve.

Serving Suggestions: Serve with fresh salad.

Variation Tip: you can use veggies of your choice.

Nutritional Information per Serving:

Calories: 162 | **Fat:** 8.1g | **Sat Fat:** 2.4g | **Carbohydrates:** 2.9g | **Fiber:** 0.6g | **Sugar:** 1.1g | **Protein:** 19.3g

Broccoli Frittata

Preparation Time: 10 minutes
Cooking Time: 13 minutes
Servings: 6

Ingredients:

- 8 eggs
- 1 tablespoon fresh cilantro, chopped
- 1 tablespoon fresh basil, chopped
- ¼ teaspoon red pepper flakes, crushed
- Salt and ground black pepper, as required
- 2 tablespoons olive oil
- 1 bunch scallions, chopped
- 1 cup broccoli, chopped finely
- ½ cup goat cheese, crumbled

Preparation:

1. Preheat the broiler of oven.
2. Arrange a rack in the upper third of oven.
3. In a bowl, add eggs, fresh herbs, red pepper flakes, salt and black pepper and beat well.
4. In an ovenproof wok, heat the oil over medium heat and sauté scallion and broccoli for about 1-2 minutes.
5. Add the egg mixture over the broccoli mixture evenly and lift the edges to let the egg mixture flow underneath.
6. Cook for about 2-3 minutes.
7. Place the cheese on top in the form of dots.
8. Now, transfer the wok under broiler and broil for about 2-3 minutes.
9. Remove the wok from oven and set aside for about five minutes.
10. Cut the frittata into desired size slices and serve.

Serving Suggestions: Serve with extra cheese sprinkling.

Variation Tip: Goat cheese can be replaced with feta cheese.

Nutritional Information per Serving:

Calories: 165 | **Fat:** 13.2g | **Sat Fat:** 4.4g | **Carbohydrates:** 2.6g | **Fiber:** 0.6g | **Sugar:** 1.4g | **Protein:** 9.7g

Kale & Mushroom Frittata

Preparation Time: 10 minutes
Cooking Time: 30 minutes
Servings: 5

Ingredients:

- 8 eggs
- ½ cup unsweetened almond milk
- Salt and ground black pepper, as required
- 1 tablespoon extra-virgin olive oil
- 1 onion, chopped
- 1 garlic clove, minced
- 1 cup fresh mushrooms, chopped
- 1½ cups fresh kale, tough ribs removed and chopped

Preparation:

1. Preheat your oven to 350° F.
2. In a large bowl, place the eggs, almond milk, salt and black pepper and beat well. Set aside.
3. In a large ovenproof wok, heat the oil over medium heat and sauté the onion and garlic for about 3-4 minutes.
4. Add the mushrooms, kale, salt and black pepper and cook for about 8-10 minutes.
5. Stir in the mushrooms and cook for about 3-4 minutes.
6. Add the kale and cook for about five minutes.
7. Place the egg mixture on top evenly and cook for about four minutes, without stirring.
8. Transfer the wok in the oven and bake for approximately 12-15 minutes or until desired doneness.
9. Remove from the oven and place the frittata side for about 3-5 minutes before serving.
10. Cut into desired sized wedges and serve.

Serving Suggestions: Serve with fresh spinach.

Variation Tip: Don't overbake the frittata.

Nutritional Information per Serving:

Calories: 148 | **Fat:** 10.2g | **Sat Fat:** 2.6g | **Carbohydrates:** 4.8g | **Fiber:** 1.2g | **Sugar:** 1.7g | **Protein:** 10.1g

Chicken & Asparagus Frittata

Preparation Time: 5 minutes
Cooking Time: 12 minutes
Servings: 4

Ingredients:

- ½ cup cooked chicken, chopped
- 1/3 cup low-fat Parmesan cheese, grated
- 6 eggs, beaten lightly
- Salt and ground black pepper, as required
- 1 teaspoon coconut oil
- ½ cup boiled asparagus, chopped
- 1 tablespoon fresh parsley, chopped

Preparation:

1. Preheat the broiler of oven.
2. In a bowl, add the cheese, eggs, salt and black pepper and beat until well-combined.
3. In a large ovenproof wok, melt coconut oil over medium-high heat and cook the chicken and asparagus for about 2-3 minutes.
4. Add the egg mixture and stir to combine.
5. Cook for about 4-5 minutes.
6. Remove from the heat and sprinkle with the parsley.
7. Now, transfer the wok under broiler and broil for about 3-4 minutes or until slightly puffed.
8. Cut into desired sized wedges and serve immediately.

Serving Suggestions: Serve with oregano on the top.

Variation Tip: Coconut oil can be replaced with oil of your choice too.

Nutritional Information per Serving:

Calories: 156 | **Fat:** 9.9g | **Sat Fat:** 4.3g | **Carbohydrates:** 1.3g | **Fiber:** 0.4g | **Sugar:** 0.8g | **Protein:** 15.4g

Chicken & Bell Pepper Muffins

Preparation Time: 15 minutes
Cooking Time: 20 minutes
Servings: 4

Ingredients:

- 8 eggs
- Salt and ground black pepper, as required
- 2 tablespoons water
- 8 ounces cooked chicken, chopped finely
- 1 cup green bell pepper, seeded and chopped
- 1 cup onion, chopped

Preparation:

1. Preheat your oven to 350° F.
2. Grease eight cups of a muffin tin.
3. In a bowl, add eggs, black pepper and water and beat until well-combined.
4. Add the chicken, bell pepper and onion and stir to combine.
5. Transfer the mixture in prepared muffin cups evenly.
6. Bake for approximately 18-20 minutes or until golden brown.
7. Remove the muffin tin from oven and place onto a wire rack to cool for about 10 minutes.
8. Carefully invert the muffins onto a platter and serve warm.

Serving Suggestions: Serve with chopped cilantro on the top.

Variation Tip: Cooked turkey meat can be used instead of chicken.

Nutritional Information per Serving:

Calories: 232 | **Fat:** 10.2g | **Sat Fat:** 6.2g | **Carbohydrates:** 5.6g | **Fiber:** 1g | **Sugar:** 3.4g | **Protein:** 28.1g

Eggs with Kale

Preparation Time: 10 minutes
Cooking Time: 22 minutes
Servings: 2

Ingredients:

- 6 cups fresh baby kale, chopped
- 2-3 tablespoons water
- 4 eggs
- Salt and ground black pepper, as required
- 2-3 tablespoons feta cheese, crumbled

Preparation:

1. Preheat your oven to 400° F.
2. Lightly grease two small baking dishes.
3. In a large frying pan, add kale and water over medium heat and cook for about 3-4 minutes.
4. Remove the frying pan from heat and drain the excess water completely.
5. Divide the kale into the prepared baking dishes evenly.
6. Carefully crack two eggs in each baking dish over kale.
7. Sprinkle with salt and black pepper and top with feta cheese evenly.
8. Arrange the baking dishes onto a large cookie sheet.
9. Bake for approximately 15-18 minutes.
10. Serve warm.

Serving Suggestions: Serve with extra cheese garnishing.

Variation Tip: You can use fresh greens of your choice in this recipe.

Nutritional Information per Serving:

Calories: 171 | **Fat:** 11.1g | **Sat Fat:** 2.4g | **Carbohydrates:** 4.3g | **Fiber:** 2g | **Sugar:** 1.4g | **Protein:** 15g

Eggs with Spinach & Tomatoes

Preparation Time: 15 minutes
Cooking Time: 25 minutes
Servings: 4

Ingredients:

- 2 tablespoons olive oil
- 1 yellow onion, chopped
- 2 garlic cloves, minced
- 1 cup tomatoes, chopped
- ½ pound fresh spinach, chopped
- 1 teaspoon ground cumin
- ¼ teaspoon red pepper flakes, crushed
- Salt and ground black pepper, as required
- 4 eggs

Preparation:

1. In a large non-stick wok, heat the olive oil over medium heat and sauté the onion for about 4-5 minutes.
2. Add in the garlic and sauté for about one minute.
3. Add the tomatoes, spices, salt and black pepper and cook for about 2-3 minutes, stirring frequently.
4. Add in the spinach and cook for about 4-5 minutes.
5. Carefully crack eggs on top of spinach mixture.
6. With the lid, cover the wok and cook for about ten minutes or until desired doneness of eggs.
7. Serve hot.

Serving Suggestions: Serve with the parsley garnishing.

Variation Tip: Adjust the ratio of spices according to your taste.

Nutritional Information per Serving:

Calories: 160 | **Fat:** 11.9g | **Sat Fat:** 4.4g | **Carbohydrates:** 7.6g | **Fiber:** 2.6g | **Sugar:** 3g | **Protein:** 8.1g

Turkey & Zucchini Muffins

Preparation Time: 15 minutes
Cooking Time: 15 minutes
Servings: 4

Ingredients:

- 4 eggs
- ¼ cup olive oil
- ¼ cup water
- 1/3 cup coconut flour
- ½ teaspoon baking powder
- ¼ teaspoon salt
- ¾ cup cooked turkey, shredded
- ¾ cup zucchini, grated
- ½ cup low-fat Parmesan cheese, shredded
- 1 tablespoon fresh oregano, minced
- 1 tablespoon fresh thyme, minced
- ¼ cup low-fat cheddar cheese, grated

Preparation:

1. Preheat your oven to 400° F.
2. Lightly grease eight cups of a muffin pan.
3. In a bowl, add eggs, oil and water and beat until well-combined
4. Add the flour, baking powder, and salt, and mix well.
5. Add the remaining ingredients and mix until just combined.
6. Place the muffin mixture into the prepared muffin cup evenly.
7. Bake for approximately 13-15 minutes or until tops become golden brown.
8. Remove muffin pan from oven and place onto a wire rack to cool for about ten minutes.
9. Invert the muffins onto a platter and serve warm.

Serving Suggestions: Serve with fresh salad.

Variation Tip: Use herbs of your choice.

Nutritional Information per Serving:

Calories: 270 | **Fat:** 21.1g | **Sat Fat:** 5.6g | **Carbohydrates:** 3.5g | **Fiber:** 1.4g | **Sugar:** 0.9g | **Protein:** 18g

Tofu & Mushroom Muffins

Preparation Time: 15 minutes
Cooking Time: 30 minutes
Servings: 6

Ingredients:

- 2 teaspoons olive oil, divided
- 1½ cups fresh mushrooms, chopped
- 1 scallion, chopped
- 1 teaspoon garlic, minced
- 1 teaspoon fresh rosemary, minced
- Ground black pepper, as required
- 1 (12.3-ounce) package lite firm silken tofu, drained
- ¼ cup unsweetened almond milk
- 2 tablespoons nutritional yeast
- 1 tablespoon arrowroot starch
- ¼ teaspoon ground turmeric

Preparation:

1. Preheat your oven to 375° F.
2. Grease a 12 cups muffin tin.
3. In a non-stick wok, heat one teaspoon of oil over medium heat and sauté scallion and garlic for about one minute.
4. Add mushrooms and sauté for about 5-7 minutes.
5. Stir in the rosemary and black pepper and remove from the heat.
6. Set aside to cool slightly.
7. In a food processor, add tofu and remaining ingredients and pulse until smooth.
8. Transfer the tofu mixture into a large bowl.
9. Fold in mushroom mixture.
10. Transfer the mixture into prepared muffin cups evenly.
11. Bake for approximately 20-22 minutes or until a toothpick inserted in the center comes out clean.
12. Remove the muffin pan from the oven and place onto a wire rack to cool for about ten minutes.
13. Carefully invert the muffins onto the wire rack and serve warm.

Serving Suggestions: Serve alongside the fresh greens.

Variation Tip: You can line the muffin tin with paper liners too.

Nutritional Information per Serving:

Calories: 74 | **Fat:** 3.6g | **Sat Fat:** 0.5g | **Carbohydrates:** 5.3g | **Fiber:** 1.4g |

Sugar: 1.1g | **Protein:** 6.2g

Strawberry & Asparagus Salad

Preparation Time: 15 minutes
Cooking Time: 5 minutes
Servings: 8

Ingredients:

- 2 pounds fresh asparagus, trimmed and sliced
- 3 cups fresh strawberries, hulled and sliced
- ¼ cup extra-virgin olive oil
- ¼ cup balsamic vinegar
- 2 tablespoons maple syrup
- Salt and ground black pepper, as required

Preparation:

1. In a pan of water, add the asparagus over medium-high heat and bring to a boil.
2. Boil the asparagus for about 2-3 minutes or until al dente.
3. Drain the asparagus and immediately transfer into a bowl of ice water to cool completely.
4. Drain the asparagus and pat dry with paper towels.
5. In a large bowl, add the asparagus and strawberries and mix.
6. In a small bowl, add the olive oil, vinegar, honey, salt and black pepper and beat until well-blended.
7. Place the dressing over the asparagus strawberry mixture and gently toss to coat.
8. Refrigerate for about one hour before serving.

Serving Suggestions: Serve with chopped nuts garnishing.

Variation Tip: Balsamic vinegar can be replaced with lemon juice too.

Nutritional Information per Serving:

Calories: 109 | **Fat:** 6.6g | **Sat Fat:** 1.1g | **Carbohydrates:** 12g | **Fiber:** 3.5g | **Sugar:** 7.8g | **Protein:** 2.9g

Berries & Spinach Salad

Preparation Time: 15 minutes
Servings: 4

Ingredients:

For Salad:

- 6 cups fresh baby spinach
- ¾ cup fresh strawberries, hulled and sliced
- ¾ cup fresh blueberries
- ¼ cup onion, sliced
- ¼ cup almond, sliced
- ¼ cup feta cheese, crumbled

For Dressing:

- 1/3 cup olive oil
- 2 tablespoons fresh lemon juice
- ¼ teaspoon liquid stevia
- 1/8 teaspoon garlic powder
- Salt, as required

Preparation:

1. For salad: In a bowl, add the spinach, berries, onion and almonds and mix.
2. For dressing: In another small bowl, add all the ingredients and beat until well-blended.
3. Place the dressing over salad and gently toss to coat well.
4. Serve immediately.

Serving Suggestions: Serve with crumbled feta cheese topping.

Variation Tip: Feel free to use berries of your choice.

Nutritional Information per Serving:

Calories: 97 | **Fat:** 5.3g | **Sat Fat:** 0.1g | **Carbohydrates:** 10g | **Fiber:** 3.1g | **Sugar:** 5.1g | **Protein:** 4.4g

Chicken & Orange Salad

Preparation Time: 15 minutes
Cooking Time: 16 minutes
Servings: 5

Ingredients:

For Chicken:

- 4 (6-ounce) boneless, skinless chicken breast halves
- Salt and ground black pepper, as required
- 2 tablespoons extra-virgin olive oil

For Salad:

- 8 cups fresh baby arugula
- 5 medium oranges, peeled and sectioned
- 1 cup onion, sliced

For Dressing:

- 2 tablespoons extra-virgin olive oil
- 2 tablespoons fresh orange juice
- 2 tablespoons balsamic vinegar
- 1½ teaspoons shallots, minced
- 1 garlic clove, minced
- Salt and ground black pepper, as required

Preparation:

1. For chicken: Season each chicken breast half with salt and black pepper evenly.
2. Place chicken over a rack set in a rimmed baking sheet.
3. Refrigerate for at least 30 minutes.
4. Remove the baking sheet from refrigerator and pat dry the chicken breast halves with paper towels.
5. Heat the oil in a 12-inch sauté pan over medium-low heat.
6. Place the chicken breast halves, smooth-side down, and cook for about 9-10 minutes without moving.
7. Flip the chicken breasts and cook for about six minutes or until cooked through.
8. Remove the sauté pan from heat and let the chicken stand in the pan for about three minutes.
9. Transfer the chicken breasts onto a cutting board for about five minutes.
10. Cut each chicken breast half into desired-sized slices.
11. For salad: Place all ingredients in a salad bowl and mix.

12. Add chicken slices and stir to combine.
13. For dressing: Place all ingredients in another bowl and beat until well-combined.
14. Place the salad onto each serving plate.
15. Drizzle with dressing and serve.

Serving Suggestions: Serve with extra oil drizzling.

Variation Tip: Fresh baby arugula can be replaced with baby greens of your choice.

Nutritional Information per Serving:

Calories: 360 | **Fat:** 15.1g | **Sat Fat:** 5.4g | **Carbohydrates:** 24g | **Fiber:** 5.4g | **Sugar:** 14g | **Protein:** 31.8g

Steak & Tomato Salad

Preparation Time: 15 minutes
Cooking Time: 15 minutes
Servings: 5
Ingredients:
For Steak:
- 2 tablespoons fresh oregano, chopped
- ½ tablespoon garlic, minced
- 1 tablespoon fresh lemon peel, grated
- ½ teaspoon red pepper flakes, crushed
- Salt and ground black pepper, as required
- 1 (1-pound) (1-inch thick) boneless beef top sirloin steak

For Salad:
- 6 cups fresh salad greens
- 2 cups cherry tomatoes, halved
- 2 tablespoons olive oil
- 2 tablespoons fresh lime juice
- Salt and ground black pepper, as required

Preparation:
1. Preheat the gas grill to medium heat.
2. Lightly grease the grill grate.
3. For steak: In a bowl, add the oregano, garlic, lemon peel, red pepper flakes, salt and black pepper and mix well.
4. Rub the steak with garlic mixture evenly.
5. Place the steak onto the grill and cook, covered for about 12-17 minutes, flipping occasionally.
6. Remove the steak from the grill and place onto a cutting board for about ten minutes.
7. Meanwhile, for salad: In a large serving bowl, place all ingredients and toss to coat well.
8. Cut the steak into bite-sized pieces.
9. Add the steak pieces into the bowl of salad and toss to coat well.
10. Serve immediately.

Serving Suggestions: Serve with feta cheese topping.
Variation Tip: Feel free to use tomatoes of your choice.
Nutritional Information per Serving:
Calories: 259 | **Fat:** 11.8g | **Sat Fat:** 2.2g | **Carbohydrates:** 9.4g | **Fiber:** 3.9g | **Sugar:** 2.6g | **Protein:** 29.4g

Salmon Salad

Preparation Time: 15 minutes
Servings: 2

Ingredients:

- 6 ounces cooked salmon, chopped
- 1 cup cucumber, sliced
- ½ cup grape tomatoes, quartered
- ¼ cup red onion, sliced
- 1 tablespoon scallion green, chopped
- 1 cup lettuce, torn
- 1 cup fresh spinach, torn
- 2 tablespoons olive oil
- 1 tablespoon fresh lemon juice
- Salt and ground black pepper, as required

Preparation:

1. In a salad bowl, place all ingredients and gently toss to coat well.
2. Serve immediately.

Serving Suggestions: Serve with fresh herbs garnishing.

Variation Tip: For best result, use freshly squeezed lemon juice.

Nutritional Information per Serving:

Calories: 263 | **Fat:** 19.6g | **Sat Fat:** 2.9g | **Carbohydrates:** 6.5g | **Fiber:** 1.6g | **Sugar:** 3.2g | **Protein:** 18g

Chicken & Kale Soup

Preparation Time: 10 minutes
Cooking Time: 15 minutes
Servings: 4

Ingredients:

- 2 tablespoons extra-virgin olive oil
- ½ of medium onion, chopped
- 3 garlic cloves, minced
- 4 cups low-sodium chicken broth
- 1 cup cooked chicken, cubed
- 1 bunch fresh kale, tough ribs removed and chopped
- 2 tablespoons fresh lemon juice
- Salt and ground black pepper, as required

Preparation:

1. In a soup pan, heat olive oil over medium-high heat and sauté the onion and garlic for about 2-3 minutes.
2. Stir in the cooked chicken and broth and bring to a gentle boil.
3. Now, adjust the heat and to low and simmer for about three minutes.
4. Stir in the kale and simmer for about five minutes or until kale is tender.
5. Stir in the lemon juice, salt and black pepper and remove from the heat.
6. Serve hot.

Serving Suggestions: Serve with low-fat Parmesan cheese garnishing.

Variation Tip: You can use greens of your choice in this soup.

Nutritional Information per Serving:

Calories: 184 | **Fat:** 10g | **Sat Fat:** 1.6g | **Carbohydrates:** 8.3g | **Fiber:** 3.9g | **Sugar:** 2.2g | **Protein:** 16.3g

Meatballs & Spinach Soup

Preparation Time: 15 minutes
Cooking Time: 25 minutes
Servings: 6

Ingredients:

For Meatballs:

- 1 pound lean ground turkey
- 1 garlic clove, minced
- 1 egg, beaten
- ¼ cup low-fat Parmesan cheese, grated
- Salt and ground black pepper, as required

For Soup:

- 1 tablespoon olive oil
- 1 small yellow onion, chopped finely
- 1 garlic clove, minced
- 6 cups low-sodium chicken broth
- 8 cups fresh baby spinach
- 2 eggs, beaten lightly

- Salt and ground black pepper, as required

Preparation:

1. For meatballs: In a bowl, add all ingredients and mix until well-combined.
2. Make equal-sized small balls from mixture.
3. In a large soup pan, heat oil over medium heat and sauté onion for about 5-6 minutes.
4. Add the garlic and sauté for about one minute.
5. Add the broth and bring to a boil.
6. Carefully place the balls in pan and bring to a boil.
7. Adjust the heat to low and cook for about ten minutes.
8. Stir in the spinach and bring the soup to a gentle simmer.
9. Simmer for about 2-3 minutes.
10. Slowly, add the beaten eggs, stirring continuously.
11. Cook for about 1-2 minutes, stirring continuously.
12. Season with salt and black pepper and remove from the heat.
13. Serve hot.

Serving Suggestions: Serve with lemon juice drizzling.

Variation Tip: For best result, use freshly grated cheese.

Nutritional Information per Serving:

Calories: 200 | **Fat:** 10.9g | **Sat Fat:** 3.3g | **Carbohydrates:** 4g | **Fiber:** 1.1g | **Sugar:** 0.8g | **Protein:** 21.7g

Beef & Bok Choy Soup

Preparation Time: 15 minutes
Cooking Time: 30 minutes
Servings: 6

Ingredients:

- 1 tablespoon olive oil
- 1 pound ground beef
- ½ pound fresh mushrooms, sliced
- 1 small yellow onion, chopped
- 1 garlic clove, minced
- 1 pound head bok choy, stalks and leaves separated and chopped
- 2 tablespoons low-sodium soy sauce
- 5 cups low-sodium chicken broth
- Ground black pepper, as required

Preparation:

1. In a large pan, heat oil over medium-high heat and cook the beef for about five minutes.
2. Add the onion, mushrooms and garlic and cook for about five minutes.
3. Add the bok choy stalks and cook for about 4-5 minutes.
4. Add soy sauce and broth and bring to a boil.
5. Adjust the heat to low. Cover and cook for about ten minutes.
6. Stir in the bok choy leaves and cook for about five minutes.
7. Stir in black pepper and serve hot.

Serving Suggestions: Serve with scallion greens topping.

Variation Tip: Remember to use low-sodium soy sauce.

Nutritional Information per Serving:

Calories: 198 | **Fat:** 7.3g | **Sat Fat:** 2.1g | **Carbohydrates:** 5.3g | **Fiber:** 1.4g | **Sugar:** 2.4g | **Protein:** 27.4g

Tofu & Mushroom Soup

Preparation Time: 15 minutes
Cooking Time: 25 minutes
Servings: 3

Ingredients:

- 3 tablespoons olive oil, divided
- 1 shallot, minced
- 1 teaspoon fresh ginger, minced
- 2 garlic cloves, minced
- 5½ ounces unsweetened coconut milk
- 1 Roma tomato, chopped
- 1 lemongrass stalk, halved crosswise
- 6 ounces fresh mushrooms, sliced
- 14 ounces extra-firm tofu, pressed, drained and cut into ½-inch cubes
- Ground black pepper, as required
- 1 scallion, sliced
- 1 tablespoon fresh cilantro

Preparation:

1. In a saucepan, heat two tablespoons of oil over medium-high heat and sauté the shallot, ginger, garlic and a pinch of salt for about 1-2 minutes.
2. Add coconut milk and remaining water and bring to a boil.
3. Add the tomato and lemongrass and stir to combine.
4. Adjust the heat to low and simmer for about 8-10 minutes.
5. Meanwhile, in a large non-stick wok, heat the remaining oil over medium-high heat and cook the mushrooms, tofu, pinch of salt and black pepper for about 5-8 minutes, stirring occasionally.
6. Remove the lemongrass stalk from pan of soup and discard it.
7. Divide the cooked mushrooms and tofu into serving bowls evenly.
8. Top with hot soup and serve with the garnishing of cilantro.

Serving Suggestions: Serve with lime juice on the top.

Variation Tip: Make sure to use unsweetened coconut milk.

Nutritional Information per Serving:

Calories: 346 | **Fat:** 29.1g | **Sat Fat:** 9.2g | **Carbohydrates:** 9.2g | **Fiber:** 1.6g | **Sugar:** 3.6g | **Protein:** 16.1g

Chicken & Spinach Stew

Preparation Time: 15 minutes
Cooking Time: 30 minutes
Servings: 8

Ingredients:

- 2 tablespoons olive oil
- 1 yellow onion, chopped
- 1 tablespoon garlic, minced
- 1 tablespoon fresh ginger, minced
- 1 teaspoon ground turmeric
- 1 teaspoon ground cumin
- 1 teaspoon paprika
- 6 (4-ounce) boneless, skinless chicken thighs, trimmed and cut into 1-inch pieces
- 4 tomatoes, chopped
- 1 (14-ounce) can unsweetened coconut milk
- Salt and ground black pepper, as required
- 3 cups fresh spinach, chopped

Preparation:

1. In a large heavy-bottomed pan, heat the oil over medium heat and sauté the onion for about 3-4 minutes.
2. Add the ginger, garlic, and spices, and sauté for about one minute.
3. Add the chicken and cook for about 4-5 minutes.
4. Add the tomatoes, coconut milk, salt, and black pepper, and bring to gentle simmer.
5. Now, adjust the heat to low and simmer, covered for about 10-15 minutes.
6. Stir in the spinach and cook for about 4–5 minutes.
7. Serve hot.

Serving Suggestions: Serve with low-fat sour cream on the top.

Variation Tip: Adjust the ratio of spices according to your taste.

Nutritional Information per Serving:

Calories: 293 | **Fat:** 17.3g | **Sat Fat:** 8.5g | **Carbohydrates:** 6.7g | **Fiber:** 1.6g | **Sugar:** 3.6g | **Protein:** 26.5g

Turkey & Mushroom Stew

Preparation Time: 15 minutes
Cooking Time: 3 hours 10 minutes
Servings: 10

Ingredients:

- 2 pounds turkey thigh and leg meat, chopped
- 2 tablespoons olive oil
- 1 garlic clove, crushed
- 12 ounces fresh button mushrooms
- 2 scallions, sliced
- 2 tablespoons fresh thyme leaves
- Salt and ground white pepper, as required
- 1 cup full-fat coconut milk
- 2 tablespoons whole-grain mustard
- 1 teaspoon xanthan gum
- ½ cup fresh parsley, roughly chopped

Preparation:

1. Heat a non-stick wok over high heat and cook the turkey meat for about 4-5 minutes or until browned completely.
2. Transfer the turkey meat into a slow cooker.
3. In the same wok, heat the oil and sauté the mushrooms and scallion for about 3-5 minutes.
4. Transfer the mushroom mixture into the slow cooker alongside the thyme, salt and black pepper.
5. In a bowl, add the coconut milk, mustard and xanthan gum and beat until well-combined.
6. Add the coconut milk mixture into the slow cooker and stir to combine well.
7. Set the slow cooker on High and cook, covered for about three hours.
8. Uncover and sir in the parsley.
9. Serve hot.

Serving Suggestions: Serve with lime juice drizzling.

Variation Tip: Use mushrooms of your choice.

Nutritional Information per Serving:

Calories: 241 | **Fat:** 16.5g | **Sat Fat:** 4.8g | **Carbohydrates:** 3.9g | **Fiber:** 1.4g | **Sugar:** 1.2g | **Protein:** 19.3g

Beef & Carrot Stew

Preparation Time: 15 minutes
Cooking Time: 55 minutes
Servings: 6

Ingredients:

- 1½ pounds beef stew meat, trimmed and chopped
- Salt and ground black pepper, as required
- 1 tablespoon olive oil
- 1 cup homemade tomato puree
- 4 cups low-sodium beef broth
- 3 carrots, peeled and sliced
- 2 garlic cloves, minced
- ½ tablespoons dried thyme
- 1 teaspoon dried parsley
- 1 teaspoon dried rosemary
- 1 tablespoon paprika
- 1 teaspoon onion powder
- 1 teaspoon garlic powder

Preparation:

1. In a bowl, add the beef cubes, salt, and black pepper and toss to coat well.
2. In a Dutch oven, heat oil over medium-high heat and cook the beef cubes for about 4–5 minutes or until browned.
3. Add in remaining ingredients and stir to combine.
4. Adjust the heat to high and bring to a boil.
5. Now, adjust the heat to low and simmer, covered for about 40–50 minutes.
6. Stir in the salt and black pepper and remove from the heat.
7. Serve hot.

Serving Suggestions: Serve with parsley garnishing.

Variation Tip: Cut the beef into equal-sized pieces.

Nutritional Information per Serving:

Calories: 278 | **Fat:** 9.7g | **Sat Fat:** 3.1g | **Carbohydrates:** 9g | **Fiber:** 2.7g | **Sugar:** 3.9g | **Protein:** 37.1g

Beef & Cabbage Stew

Preparation Time: 15 minutes
Cooking Time: 1 hour 50 minutes
Servings: 8

Ingredients:

- 2 pounds beef stew meat, trimmed and cubed into 1-inch size
- 1 1/3 cups hot low-sodium chicken broth
- 2 yellow onions, chopped
- 2 bay leaves
- 1 teaspoon Greek seasoning
- Salt and ground black pepper, as required
- 3 celery stalks, chopped
- 1 (8-ounce) package shredded cabbage
- 1 (6-ounce) can sugar-free tomato sauce
- 1 (8-ounce) can sugar-free whole plum tomatoes, chopped roughly with liquid

Preparation:

1. Heat a large non-stick pan over medium-high heat and cook the beef for about 4-5 minutes or until browned.
2. Drain excess grease from the pan.
3. Stir in the broth, onion, bay leaves, Greek seasoning, salt and black pepper and bring to a boil.
4. Adjust the heat to low and cook, covered for about 1¼ hours.
5. Stir in the celery and cabbage and cook, covered for about 30 minutes.
6. Stir in the tomato sauce and chopped plum tomatoes and cook, uncovered for about 15-20 minutes.
7. Stir in the salt and remove from heat.
8. Discard bay leaves and serve hot.

Serving Suggestions: Serve with fresh herbs garnishing.

Variation Tip: Use sugar-free tomato sauce.

Nutritional Information per Serving:

Calories: 243 | **Fat:** 7.3g | **Sat Fat:** 2.7g | **Carbohydrates:** 7g | **Fiber:** 2.1g | **Sugar:** 2.8g | **Protein:** 36g

Chicken Burgers

Preparation Time: 15 minutes
Cooking Time: 10 minutes
Servings: 4

Ingredients:

For Burgers:

- 1¼ pounds ground chicken
- 1 egg
- ½ yellow onion, grated
- Salt and ground black pepper, as required
- 1 teaspoon dried thyme
- 2 tablespoons olive oil

For Serving:

- 4 cups lettuce, torn
- 1 cucumber, chopped

Preparation:

1. In a bowl, add all the ingredients and mix until well-combined.
2. Make eight small equal-sized patties from the mixture.
3. In a large frying pan, heat the oil over medium heat and cook the patties for about 4-5 minutes per side or until done completely.
4. Divide the lettuce and cucumber onto serving plates and top each with two burgers.
5. Serve hot.

Serving Suggestions: Serve with the sour cream topping.

Variation Tip: Use high-quality ground chicken.

Nutritional Information per Serving:

Calories: 370 | **Fat:** 18.8g | **Sat Fat:** 4.3g | **Carbohydrates:** 5.9g | **Fiber:** 1.1g | **Sugar:** 2.5g | **Protein:** 42.3g

Turkey Burgers

Preparation Time: 15 minutes
Cooking Time: 6 minutes
Servings: 2

Ingredients:

For Burgers:

- 8 ounces lean ground turkey
- Salt and ground black pepper, as required
- 1 ounce part-skim Mozzarella cheese, cubed
- 1 tablespoon olive oil

For Serving:

- 2 cups fresh baby spinach
- 1 small cucumber, chopped

Preparation:

1. In a bowl, add the turkey, salt and black pepper and mix until well-combined.
2. Make two equal-sized patties from the mixture.
3. Place mozzarella cubes over each patty and with your fingers, press inside.
4. In a wok, heat oil over medium heat and cook the patties for about 2-3 minutes per side.
5. Serve immediately alongside the spinach and cucumber.

Serving Suggestions: Serve alongside the sugar-free ketchup.

Variation Tip: Don't overmix the turkey mixture.

Nutritional Information per Serving:

Calories: 351 | **Fat:** 22.2g | **Sat Fat:** 4.7g | **Carbohydrates:** 7.1g | **Fiber:** 1.4g | **Sugar:** 2.6g | **Protein:** 36.9g

Beef Burgers

Preparation Time: 10 minutes
Cooking Time: 20 minutes
Servings: 4

Ingredients:

For Burgers:

- 1 pound lean ground beef
- ¼ cup fresh parsley, chopped
- ¼ cup fresh cilantro, chopped
- 1 tablespoon fresh ginger, chopped
- 1 teaspoon ground cumin
- 1 teaspoon ground coriander
- ½ teaspoon ground cinnamon
- Salt and ground black pepper, as required

For Salad:

- 6 cups fresh baby arugula
- 2 cups cherry tomatoes, quartered
- 1 tablespoon fresh lemon juice
- 1 tablespoon extra-virgin olive oil

Preparation:

1. In a bowl, add the beef, ¼ cup of parsley, cilantro, ginger, spices, salt and black pepper and mix until well-combined.
2. Make four equal-sized patties from the mixture.
3. Heat a greased grill pan over medium-high heat and cook the patties for about three minutes per side or until desired doneness.
4. Meanwhile, in a bowl, add arugula, tomatoes, lemon juice and oil and toss to coat well.
5. Divide the salad onto serving plates and top each with one patty.
6. Serve immediately.

Serving Suggestions: Serve alongside your favorite dipping sauce.

Variation Tip: You can adjust the ratio of spices according to your taste.

Nutritional Information per Serving:

Calories: 274 | **Fat:** 11.2g | **Sat Fat:** 3.3g | **Carbohydrates:** 6.4g | **Fiber:** 2.1g | **Sugar:** 3.2g | **Protein:** 36.3g

Salmon Burgers

Preparation Time: 15 minutes
Cooking Time: 20 minutes
Servings: 4

Ingredients:

- 1 egg
- 3 tablespoons sugar-free ranch dressing
- 1 (14-ounce) can pink salmon, drained and bones removed
- 2 ounces smoked salmon, chopped roughly
- 1/3 cup almond flour
- 2 tablespoons fresh parsley, chopped
- 1 teaspoon Cajun seasoning
- 2 tablespoons avocado oil
- 6 cups fresh baby spinach

Preparation:

1. In a bowl, add the egg and ranch dressing and beat until well combined.
2. Add the remaining ingredients except for spinach and gently, mix until well combined.
3. Make eight equal-sized patties from the mixture.
4. In a non-stick wok, heat oil over medium heat and cook the patties in two batches for about 3-5 minutes per side or until golden brown.
5. Divide the baby spinach onto serving plates and top each with two burgers.
6. Serve immediately.

Serving Suggestions: Serve with scallion greens garnishing.

Variation Tip: Make sure to use sugar-free ranch dressing.

Nutritional Information per Serving:

Calories: 256 | **Fat:** 14.1g | **Sat Fat:** 1.2g | **Carbohydrates:** 6.7g | **Fiber:** 2.4g | **Sugar:** 1.2g | **Protein:** 24.7g

Chicken with Zucchini

Preparation Time: 15 minutes
Cooking Time: 17 minutes
Servings: 6

Ingredients:

- 2 tablespoons olive oil, divided
- 1½ pounds skinless, boneless chicken breasts, cut into bite-sized pieces
- Salt and ground black pepper, as required
- 2 garlic cloves, minced
- 1½ pounds zucchini, sliced
- 2 tablespoons fresh lemon juice
- 1 teaspoon fresh lemon zest, grated finely
- 2 tablespoons fresh parsley, minced

Preparation:

1. In a wok, heat one tablespoon of oil over medium heat and stir fry chicken for about 6-8 minutes or until golden brown from all sides.
2. Transfer the chicken onto a plate.
3. In the same wok, heat remaining oil over medium heat and sauté garlic for about one minute.
4. Add the squash slices and cook for about 5-6 minutes,
5. Stir in the chicken and cook for about two minutes.
6. Stir in the lemon juice, zest and parsley and remove from heat.

Serving Suggestions: Serve alongside fresh salad.

Variation Tip: You can use yellow squash instead of zucchini.

Nutritional Information per Serving:

Calories: 203 | **Fat:** 9g | **Sat Fat:** 2.3g | **Carbohydrates:** 4.4g | **Fiber:** 1.4g | **Sugar:** 2.1g | **Protein:** 26.8g

Green Chicken Curry

Preparation Time: 15 minutes
Cooking Time: 30 minutes
Servings: 4

Ingredients:

- 1 pound skinless, boneless chicken breasts, cubed
- 1 tablespoon olive oil
- 2 tablespoons green curry paste
- 1 cup unsweetened coconut milk
- 1 cup low-sodium chicken broth
- 1 cup asparagus spears, trimmed
- 1 cup green beans, trimmed
- Salt and ground black pepper, as required
- ¼ cup fresh cilantro leaves, chopped

Preparation:

1. In a wok, heat oil over medium heat and sauté the curry paste for about 1-2 minutes.
2. Add the chicken and cook for about 8-10 minutes.
3. Add coconut milk and broth and bring to a boil.
4. Adjust the heat to low and cook for about 8-10 minutes.
5. Add asparagus, green beans, salt and black pepper and cook for about 4-5 minutes or until desired doneness.
6. Serve hot.

Serving Suggestions: Serve with lime juice drizzling.

Variation Tip: Feel free to add veggies of your choice.

Nutritional Information per Serving:

Calories: 331 | **Fat:** 20.3g | **Sat Fat:** 9.5g | **Carbohydrates:** 7.2g | **Fiber:** 1.7g | **Sugar:** 2.5g | **Protein:** 8.2g

Turkey with Peas

Preparation Time: 15 minutes
Cooking Time: 40 minutes
Servings: 6

Ingredients:

- 2 tablespoons extra virgin olive oil
- 1 pound lean ground turkey
- 1 large white onion, chopped finely
- 2 garlic cloves, minced
- ½ tablespoon fresh ginger, minced
- 1 teaspoon ground coriander
- 1 teaspoon ground cumin
- ¼ teaspoon chili powder
- 2 medium tomatoes, seeded and chopped
- ½ cup low-sodium chicken broth
- Salt and ground black pepper, as required
- 2 cups fresh peas, shelled
- 2 tablespoons fresh cilantro, chopped

Preparation:

1. In a wok, heat the oil over medium heat and cook the turkey for about 4-5 minutes or until browned completely.
2. With a slotted spoon, transfer the turkey into a large bowl.
3. In the same wok, add the onion and sauté for about 4-6 minutes.
4. Add the garlic, ginger, coriander, cumin and chili powder and sauté for about one minute.
5. Add the tomatoes and cook for about 2-3 minutes, crushing completely with the back of the spoon.
6. Stir in the cooked turkey, broth, salt and black pepper and bring to a boil.
7. Adjust the heat to medium-low and simmer, covered for about 8-10 minutes, stirring occasionally.
8. Stir in peas and cook for about 15-20 minutes.
9. Serve hot with the garnishing of cilantro.

Serving Suggestions: Serve with julienned fresh ginger topping.

Variation Tip: You can use frozen peas instead of fresh peas.

Nutritional Information per Serving:

Calories: 211 | **Fat:** 10.5g | **Sat Fat:** 2.4g | **Carbohydrates:** 11.9g | **Fiber:** 3.7g | **Sugar:** 4.9g | **Protein:** 18.5g

Beef with Broccoli

Preparation Time: 15 minutes
Cooking Time: 20 minutes
Servings: 4

Ingredients:

- 16 ounces sirloin steak, trimmed and cut into thin strips
- Ground black pepper, as required
- 2 tablespoons olive oil, divided
- 2 garlic cloves, mince
- 1 Serrano pepper, seeded and chopped finely
- 2½ cups broccoli florets
- 2 tablespoons low-sodium soy sauce
- 2 tablespoons fresh lime juice

Preparation:

1. Season the steak slices with black pepper evenly.
2. In a cast-iron wok, heat one tablespoon of oil over medium heat and cook the steak slices for about 6-8 minutes or until browned from all sides.
3. With a slotted spoon, transfer the steak slices onto a plate.
4. In the same wok, heat the remaining oil over medium heat and sauté the garlic and Serrano pepper for about one minute.
5. Add in broccoli and stir fry for about 2-3 minutes.
6. Stir in cooked steak slices, soy sauce and lime juice and cook for about 3-4 minutes.
7. Serve hot.

Serving Suggestions: Serve with fresh herbs garnishing.

Variation Tip: Choose a steak that is as uniform as possible in its thickness.

Nutritional Information per Serving:

Calories: 296 | **Fat:** 14.3g | **Sat Fat:** 3.4g | **Carbohydrates:** 4.9g | **Fiber:** 1.6g | **Sugar:** 1.6g | **Protein:** 36.6g

Beef with Bell Peppers

Preparation Time: 15 minutes
Cooking Time: 10 minutes
Servings: 4

Ingredients:

- 1 tablespoon olive oil
- 1 pound flank steak, cut into thin slices across the grain diagonally
- 3 small multi-colored bell peppers, seeded and cut into thin strips
- 1 tablespoon fresh ginger, minced
- 3 tablespoons low-sodium soy sauce
- 1½ tablespoons balsamic vinegar
- 2 teaspoons Sriracha

Preparation:

1. In a non-stick wok, heat the oil over medium-high heat and sear the steak slices for about two minutes.
2. Add the bell peppers and cook for about 2-3 minutes, stirring continuously.
3. With a slotted spoon, transfer the beef mixture into a bowl.
4. In the wok, add the remaining ingredients over medium heat and bring to a boil.
5. Cook for about one minute, stirring frequently.
6. Add the beef mixture and cook for about 1-2 minutes.
7. Serve hot.

Serving Suggestions: Serve with sesame seeds garnishing.

Variation Tip: Adjust the ratio of Sriracha according to your spice tolerance.

Nutritional Information per Serving:

Calories: 274 | **Fat:** 13.1g | **Sat Fat:** 2.9g | **Carbohydrates:** 5g | **Fiber:** 1.2g | **Sugar:** 2.3g | **Protein:** 32.9g

Beef with Carrot & Kale

Preparation Time: 15 minutes
Cooking Time: 12 minutes
Servings: 4

Ingredients:

- 2 tablespoons olive oil
- 4 garlic cloves, minced
- 1 pound beef sirloin steak, cut into bite-sized pieces
- Ground black pepper, as required
- 1 ½ cups carrots, peeled and cut into matchsticks
- 1 ½ cups fresh kale, tough ribs removed and chopped
- 3 tablespoons low-sodium soy sauce

Preparation:

1. In a wok, heat the oil over medium heat and sauté the garlic for about one minute.
2. Add the beef and black pepper and stir to combine.
3. Adjust the heat to medium-high and cook for about 3-4 minutes or until browned from all sides.
4. Add the carrot, kale and soy sauce and cook for about 4-5 minutes.
5. Stir in the black pepper and remove from the heat.
6. Serve hot.

Serving Suggestions: Serve with scallion garnishing.

Variation Tip: You can use tamari instead of soy sauce.

Nutritional Information per Serving:

Calories: 308 | **Fat:** 14.1g | **Sat Fat:** 3.7g | **Carbohydrates:** 7g | **Fiber:** 1g | **Sugar:** 2.8g | **Protein:** 36.4g

Beef Chili

Preparation Time: 15 minutes
Cooking Time: 1¾ hours
Servings: 10

Ingredients:

- 2 tablespoons olive oil
- 3 pounds ground beef
- 1 cup yellow onion, chopped finely
- ½ cup celery, chopped finely
- 1 cup bell pepper, seeded and chopped finely
- 1 (15-ounce) can crushed tomatoes with juice
- 1 ½ cups tomato juice
- 1 ½ teaspoons Worcestershire sauce
- ½ teaspoon dried oregano
- 3 tablespoons red chili powder
- 1 teaspoon ground cumin
- 1 teaspoon garlic powder
- 1 teaspoon salt
- ½ teaspoon ground black pepper

Preparation:

1. In a saucepan, heat oil over medium-high heat and cook the beef for about 8-10 minutes or until browned.
2. Drain the grease from pan, leaving about 2 tablespoons inside.
3. In the pan, add the onions, celery and bell peppers over medium-high heat and cook for about five minutes, stirring frequently.
4. Add the tomatoes, tomato juice, Worcestershire sauce, oregano and spices and stir to combine.
5. Adjust the heat to low and simmer, covered for about 1-1½ hours, stirring occasionally.
6. Serve hot.

Serving Suggestions: Serve with low-fat sour cream topping.

Variation Tip: Olive oil can be replaced with canola oil.

Nutritional Information per Serving:

Calories: 317 | **Fat:** 11.8g | **Sat Fat:** 3.7g | **Carbohydrates:** 8.4g | **Fiber:** 2.8g | **Sugar:** 4.9g | **Protein:** 43.2g

Ground Beef with Veggies

Preparation Time: 15 minutes
Cooking Time: 25 minutes
Servings: 4

Ingredients:

- 1 pound lean ground beef
- 2 tablespoons extra-virgin olive oil
- 2 garlic cloves, minced
- ½ of yellow onion, chopped
- 2 cups fresh mushrooms, sliced
- 1 cup fresh spinach, chopped
- ¼ cup low-sodium beef broth
- 2 tablespoons balsamic vinegar
- 2 tablespoons fresh parsley, chopped

Preparation:

1. Heat a large non-stick wok over medium-high heat and cook the ground beef for about 8-10 minutes, breaking up the chunks with a wooden spoon.
2. With a slotted spoon, transfer the beef into a bowl.
3. In the same wok, add the onion and garlic for about three minutes.
4. Add the mushrooms and cook for about five minutes.
5. Add the cooked beef, spinach, broth and vinegar and bring to a boil.
6. Adjust the heat to medium-low and simmer for about three minutes.
7. Stir in parsley and serve immediately.

Serving Suggestions: Serve with fresh lime juice drizzling.

Variation Tip: You can use any kind of fresh mushrooms in this dish.

Nutritional Information per Serving:

Calories: 216 | **Fat:** 14.2g | **Sat Fat:** 3.7g | **Carbohydrates:** 3.5g | **Fiber:** 0.9g | **Sugar:** 1.3g | **Protein:** 36.2g

Salmon with Cauliflower Mash

Preparation Time: 15 minutes
Cooking Time: 20 minutes
Servings: 4

Ingredients:

For Cauliflower Mash:

- 1 pound cauliflower, cut into florets
- 1 tablespoon extra-virgin olive oil
- 3 garlic cloves, minced
- 1 teaspoon fresh thyme leaves
- Salt and ground black pepper, as required

For Salmon:

- 1 (1-inch) piece fresh ginger, grated finely
- 1 tablespoon honey
- 1 tablespoon fresh lemon juice
- 1 tablespoon Dijon mustard
- 2 tablespoons olive oil
- 4 (6-ounce) salmon fillets
- 2 tablespoons fresh parsley, chopped

Preparation:

1. For cauliflower mash: In a large saucepan of water, arrange a steamer basket and bring to a boil.
2. Place the cauliflower florets in the steamer basket and steam, covered for about ten minutes.
3. Drain the cauliflower and set aside.
4. In a small frying pan, heat the oil over medium heat and sauté the garlic for about two minutes.
5. Remove the frying pan from heat and transfer the garlic oil in a large food processor.
6. Add the cauliflower, thyme, salt and black pepper and pulse until smooth.
7. Transfer the cauliflower mash into a bowl and set aside.
8. Meanwhile, in a bowl, mix together ginger, honey, lemon juice and Dijon mustard. Set aside.
9. In a non-stick wok, heat olive oil over medium-high heat and cook the salmon fillets for about 3-4 minutes per side.
10. Stir in the honey mixture and immediately remove from heat.
11. Divide the warm cauliflower mash onto serving plates.
12. Top each plate with one salmon fillet and serve.

Serving Suggestions: Serve with lemon juice drizzling.

Variation Tip: Honey can be replaced with maple syrup.

Nutritional Information per Serving:

Calories: 308 | **Fat:** 14.4g | **Sat Fat:** 5.4g | **Carbohydrates:** 11g | **Fiber:** 3.2g | **Sugar:** 7g | **Protein:** 35.7g

Tilapia with Asparagus

Preparation Time: 10 minutes
Cooking Time: 6 minutes
Servings: 5

Ingredients:

- 2 tablespoons olive oil
- 5 (5-ounce) tilapia fillets
- 3 garlic cloves, minced
- 1 tablespoon fresh ginger, minced
- 2-3 tablespoons chicken broth
- Salt and ground black pepper, as required
- 1½ pounds fresh asparagus

Preparation:

1. In a non-stick wok, heat the oil over medium heat and cook the tilapia fillets for about three minutes.
2. Flip the side and stir in the garlic and ginger.
3. Cook for about 1-2 minutes.
4. Add the broth and cook for about 2-3 more minutes.
5. Remove from heat and serve hot.
6. Meanwhile, in a pan of boiling water, add asparagus and cook for about 4-5 minutes.
7. Drain the asparagus well.
8. Divide the asparagus onto serving plates evenly and top each with one tilapia fillet and serve.

Serving Suggestions: Serve with fresh herbs garnishing.

Variation Tip: Don't overcook the fish.

Nutritional Information per Serving:

Calories: 172 | **Fat:** 7g | **Sat Fat:** 1.4g | **Carbohydrates:** 1.4g | **Fiber:** 0.2g | **Sugar:** 0.1g | **Protein:** 26.7g

Shrimp with Zoodles

Preparation Time: 20 minutes
Cooking Time: 8 minutes
Servings: 4

Ingredients:

- 2 tablespoons olive oil
- 1 garlic clove, minced
- ¼ teaspoon red pepper flakes, crushed
- 1 pound shrimp, peeled and deveined
- Salt and ground black pepper, as required
- 1/3 cup low-sodium chicken broth
- 2 medium zucchinis, spiralized with blade C

Preparation:

1. In a non-stick wok, heat olive oil over medium heat and sauté garlic and red pepper flakes for about one minute.
2. Add the shrimp, salt and black pepper and cook for about one minute per side.
3. Add the broth and zucchini noodles and cook for about 3-4 minutes.
4. Serve hot.

Serving Suggestions: Serve with Parmesan cheese garnishing.

Variation Tip: Don't use shrimp with any smell.

Nutritional Information per Serving:

Calories: 213 | **Fat:** 9.1g | **Sat Fat:** 1.8g | **Carbohydrates:** 5.4g | **Fiber:** 1.1g | **Sugar:** 1.7g | **Protein:** 27.3g

Shrimp with Spinach

Preparation Time: 15 minutes
Cooking Time: 10 minutes
Servings: 4

Ingredients:

- 3 tablespoons olive oil
- 1 pound medium shrimp, peeled and deveined
- 1 medium onion, chopped
- 4 garlic cloves, chopped finely
- 1 pound fresh spinach, chopped
- ¼ cup chicken broth
- Salt and ground black pepper, as required

Preparation:

1. In a non-stick wok, heat one tablespoon of the oil over medium-high heat and cook the shrimp for about two minutes per side.
2. With a slotted spoon, transfer the shrimp onto a plate.
3. In the same wok, heat the remaining oil over medium heat and sauté the garlic and red chili for about one minute.
4. Add the spinach and broth and cook for about 3-4 minutes, stirring occasionally.
5. Stir in the cooked shrimp, salt and black pepper and cook for about one minute.
6. Serve hot.

Serving Suggestions: Serve with lemon zest garnishing.

Variation Tip: Use raw shrimp for this recipe.

Nutritional Information per Serving:

Calories: 240 | **Fat:** 12.3g | **Sat Fat:** 4.1g | **Carbohydrates:** 7.7g | **Fiber:** 3.1g | **Sugar:** 1.7g | **Protein:** 28.2g

Tofu with Broccoli

Preparation Time: 20 minutes
Cooking Time: 25 minutes
Servings: 4
Ingredients:
For Tofu:
- 14 ounces firm tofu, drained, pressed and cut into 1-inch slices
- 1/3 cup arrowroot starch, divided
- ¼ cup olive oil
- 1 teaspoon fresh ginger, grated
- 1 medium onion, sliced thinly
- 3 tablespoons low-sodium soy sauce
- 2 tablespoons balsamic vinegar
- 1 tablespoon maple syrup
- ½ cup water

For Steamed Broccoli:
- 2 cups broccoli florets

Preparation:
1. In a shallow bowl, place ¼ cup of the arrowroot starch.
2. Add the tofu cubes and coat with arrowroot starch.
3. In a cast-iron wok, heat the olive oil over medium heat and cook the tofu cubes for about 8-10 minutes or until golden from all sides.
4. With a slotted spoon, transfer the tofu cubes onto a plate. Set aside.
5. In the same wok, add ginger and sauté for about one minute.
6. Add the onions and sauté for about 2-3 minutes.
7. Add the soy sauce, vinegar and maple syrup and bring to a gentle simmer.
8. In the meantime, in a small bowl, dissolve the remaining arrowroot starch in water.
9. Slowly, add the arrowroot starch mixture into the sauce, stirring continuously.
10. Stir in the cooked tofu and cook for about one minute.
11. Meanwhile, in a large pan of water, arrange a steamer basket and bring to a boil.
12. Adjust the heat to medium-low.
13. Place the broccoli florets in the steamer basket and steam, covered for about 5-6 minutes.
14. Remove from the heat and drain the broccoli completely.
15. Transfer the broccoli into the wok of tofu and stir to combine.
16. Serve hot.

Serving Suggestions: Serve with sesame seeds garnishing.
Variation Tip: Use freshly grated ginger.
Nutritional Information per Serving:
Calories: 230 | **Fat:** 17g | **Sat Fat:** 3.4g | **Carbohydrates:** 13g | **Fiber:** 2.9g | **Sugar:** 6.3g | **Protein:** 10.9g

Tofu with Kale

Preparation Time: 15 minutes
Cooking Time: 10 minutes
Servings: 2

Ingredients:

- 1 tablespoon extra-virgin olive oil
- ½ pound tofu, pressed, drained and cubed
- 1 teaspoon fresh ginger, minced
- 1 garlic clove, minced
- ¼ teaspoon red pepper flakes, crushed
- 6 ounces fresh kale, tough ribs removed and chopped finely
- 1 tablespoon low-sodium soy sauce

Preparation:

1. In a large non-stick wok, heat olive oil over medium-high heat and stir-fry the tofu for about 3-4 minutes.
2. Add the ginger, garlic and red pepper flakes and cook for about one minute, stirring continuously.
3. Stir in the kale and soy sauce and stir-fry for about 4-5 minutes.
4. Serve hot.

Serving Suggestions: Serve with scallion garnishing.

Variation Tip: Use low-sodium soy sauce.

Nutritional Information per Serving:

Calories: 191 | **Fat:** 12.4g | **Sat Fat:** 2g | **Carbohydrates:** 12g | **Fiber:** 3.4g | **Sugar:** 1.3g | **Protein:** 13.2g

Tofu with Brussels Sprout

Preparation Time: 15 minutes
Cooking Time: 15 minutes
Servings: 3

Ingredients:

- 1½ tablespoons olive oil, divided
- 8 ounces extra-firm tofu, drained, pressed and cut into slices
- 2 garlic cloves, chopped
- 1/3 cup pecans, toasted and chopped
- 1 tablespoon unsweetened applesauce
- ¼ cup fresh cilantro, chopped
- 1 pound Brussels sprouts, trimmed and cut into wide ribbons

Preparation:

1. In a non-stick wok, heat ½ tablespoon of oil over medium heat and sauté the tofu and for about 6-7 minutes or until golden brown.
2. Add the garlic and pecans and sauté for about one minute.
3. Add the applesauce and cook for about two minutes.
4. Stir in the cilantro and remove from heat.
5. Transfer tofu into a plate and set aside.
6. In the same wok, heat the remaining oil over medium-high heat and cook the brussels sprouts for about five minutes.
7. Stir in the tofu and remove from the heat.
8. Serve immediately.

Serving Suggestions: Serve with fresh salad.

Variation Tip: Remember to drain the tofu.

Nutritional Information per Serving:

Calories: 238 | **Fat:** 17.8g | **Sat Fat:** 2g | **Carbohydrates:** 12g | **Fiber:** 4.8g | **Sugar:** 4.5g | **Protein:** 11.8g

Tofu with Peas

Preparation Time: 15 minutes
Cooking Time: 20 minutes
Servings: 5

Ingredients:

- 2 tablespoons olive oil, divided
- 1 (16-ounce) package extra-firm tofu, drained, pressed and cubed
- 1 cup yellow onion, chopped
- 1 tablespoon fresh ginger, minced
- 2 garlic cloves, minced
- 1 tomato, chopped finely
- 2 cups frozen peas, thawed
- ¼ cup water
- 2 tablespoons fresh cilantro, chopped

Preparation:

1. In a non-stick wok, heat one tablespoon of the oil over medium-high heat and cook the tofu for about 4-5 minutes or until browned completely, stirring occasionally.
2. Transfer the tofu into a bowl.
3. In the same wok, heat the remaining oil over medium heat and sauté the onion for about 3-4 minutes.
4. Add the ginger and garlic and sauté for about one minute.
5. Add the tomatoes and cook for about 4-5 minutes, crushing with the back of a spoon.
6. Stir in the peas and broth and cook for about 2-3 minutes.
7. Stir in the tofu and cook for about 1-2 minutes.
8. Serve hot with the garnishing of cilantro.

Serving Suggestions: Serve with lemon juice drizzling.

Variation Tip: Make sure to thaw the peas.

Nutritional Information per Serving:

Calories: 198 | **Fat:** 11.2g | **Sat Fat:** 1.3g | **Carbohydrates:** 14.7g | **Fiber:** 4.2g | **Sugar:** 4.8g | **Protein:** 12.6g

Chicken with Bell Peppers & Onion

Preparation Time: 15 minutes
Cooking Time: 20 minutes
Servings: 6

Ingredients:

- 3 tablespoons olive oil, divided
- 3 bell peppers, seeded and sliced
- 1 medium onion, sliced
- 16 ounces skinless, boneless chicken breasts, cut into thin slices
- 1 teaspoon dried oregano, crushed
- ¼ teaspoon garlic powder
- ¼ teaspoon ground cumin
- Salt and ground black pepper, as required
- ¼ cup low-sodium chicken broth

Preparation:

1. Heat one tablespoon of the olive oil in a wok over medium-high heat and cook the bell peppers and onion slices for about 4-5 minutes.
2. With a slotted spoon, transfer the pepper mixture onto a plate.
3. In the same wok, heat the remaining oil over medium-high heat and cook the chicken for about eight minutes, stirring frequently.
4. Stir in the thyme, spices, salt, black pepper, and broth, and bring to a boil.
5. Add in the pepper mixture and stir to combine.
6. Immediately adjust the heat to medium and cook for about 3-5 minutes or until all the liquid is absorbed, stirring occasionally.
7. Serve immediately.

Serving Suggestions: Serve with lemon juice drizzling.

Variation Tip: You can use multi-colored bell peppers.

Nutritional Information per Serving:

Calories: 246 | **Fat:** 13.6g | **Sat Fat:** 4.6g | **Carbohydrates:** 5.6g | **Fiber:** 1.7g | **Sugar:** 2.6g | **Protein:** 25.2g

Steak with Green Beans

Preparation Time: 15 minutes
Cooking Time: 10 minutes
Servings: 4

Ingredients:

- ¼ cup low-sodium soy sauce
- 2 tablespoons balsamic vinegar
- ½ teaspoon arrowroot starch
- 1 tablespoon olive oil
- ¾ pound flank steak, trimmed and thinly sliced
- 1 pound green beans, trimmed
- 2 garlic cloves, minced
- 2 teaspoon fresh ginger, minced

Preparation:

1. For sauce: In a small bowl, add the soy sauce, vinegar and arrowroot starch and mix well. Set aside.
2. In a non-stick wok, heat the oil over medium-high heat and cook the steak slices for about 1-2 minutes per side.
3. With a slotted spoon, transfer the steak slices onto a plate.
4. In the same wok, place the green beans and cook for about 2-3 minutes, stirring occasionally.
5. Add in ginger and garlic and cook for about one minute, stirring continuously.
6. Stir in the sauce and steak slices and cook for about 1-2 minutes, stirring continuously.
7. Serve hot.

Serving Suggestions: Serve with sesame seeds garnishing.

Variation Tip: Cut the steak into equal-sized thin slices.

Nutritional Information per Serving:

Calories: 246 | **Fat:** 10.8g | **Sat Fat:** 2.4g | **Carbohydrates:** 10g | **Fiber:** 4.1g | **Sugar:** 1.9g | **Protein:** 26.7g

Steak with Mushrooms

Preparation Time: 15 minutes
Cooking Time: 18 minutes
Servings: 2

Ingredients:

For Steak:

- 2 teaspoons extra-virgin olive oil
- 2 (4-ounce) strip steaks, trimmed
- Salt and ground black pepper, as required

For Mushroom Sauce:

- 2 tablespoons extra-virgin olive oil
- 1/3 cup fresh shiitake mushrooms, sliced
- ½ of shallot, sliced
- 1 garlic clove, peeled
- ¾ cup low-sodium beef broth
- 2 tablespoons fresh parsley, chopped
- Salt and ground black pepper, as required

Preparation:

1. In a heavy-bottomed skillet, heat the oil over high heat and cook the steaks with salt and black pepper for about 3-4 minutes per side.
2. With a slotted spoon, transfer the steaks onto a plate.
3. With a piece of foil, cover the steaks to keep warm.
4. In the same wok, heat the remaining oil over medium-low heat and cook the mushrooms, shallot and garlic for about 5-6 minutes, stirring frequently.
5. Add in the broth and cook for about 3-4 minute, stirring frequently.
6. Stir in the parsley salt and black pepper and remove from the heat.
7. Divide the steaks onto serving plates and serve with the topping of mushroom sauce.

Serving Suggestions: Serve with fresh herbs garnishing.

Variation Tip: The steak should have good color and appear moist but not wet.

Nutritional Information per Serving:

Calories: 292 | **Fat:** 20.4g | **Sat Fat:** 6.1g | **Carbohydrates:** 5.5g | **Fiber:** 0.4g | **Sugar:** 2.4g | **Protein:** 23.4g

Scallops Salad

Preparation Time: 15 minutes
Cooking Time: 6 minutes
Servings: 4

Ingredients:

For Scallops:

- 1¼ pounds fresh sea scallops, side muscles removed
- Salt and ground black pepper, as required
- 2 tablespoons olive oil
- 1 garlic clove, minced

For Salad:

- 4 cups fresh salad greens
- 2 oranges, peeled and sectioned
- ¼ cup yellow grape tomatoes, halved
- ¼ cup red grape tomatoes, halved
- ¼ cup onion, sliced
- 2 tablespoons olive oil
- 2 tablespoons fresh lemon juice
- Salt and ground black pepper, as required

Preparation:

1. Sprinkle the scallops evenly with salt and black pepper.
2. In a wok, heat oil over medium-high heat and cook the scallops for about 2-3 minutes per side.
3. Meanwhile, for salad: In a bowl, add all ingredients and toss to coat well.
4. Divide salad onto serving plates.
5. Top each plate with scallops and serve.

Serving Suggestions: Serve with feta cheese garnishing.

Variation Tip: Feel free to use greens of your choice.

Nutritional Information per Serving:

Calories: 275 | **Fat:** 11.9g | **Sat Fat:** 1.7g | **Carbohydrates:** 17.8g | **Fiber:** 3g | **Sugar:** 10.2g | **Protein:** 25.3g

Shrimp Salad

Preparation Time: 15 minutes
Cooking Time: 3 minutes
Servings: 4

Ingredients:

- 1 pound shrimp, peeled and deveined
- 1 lemon, quartered
- Salt, as required
- 2 tablespoons olive oil
- 2 teaspoons fresh lemon juice
- Ground black pepper, as required
- 1 large avocado, peeled, pitted and chopped
- ½ cup cherry tomatoes, halved
- 4 cups fresh lettuce, torn

Preparation:

1. In a pan of boiling water, add the quartered lemon and a little salt.
2. Then, add the shrimp and cook for about 2-3 minutes or until pink and opaque.
3. With a slotted spoon, transfer the shrimp into a bowl of ice water to stop the cooking process.
4. Drain the shrimp completely and then pat dry with paper towels.
5. In a small bowl, add the oil, lemon juice, salt, and black pepper, and beat until well-blended.
6. Divide the shrimp, avocado, tomato and lettuce onto serving plates.
7. Drizzle with oil mixture and serve.

Serving Suggestions: Serve with parsley on the top.

Variation Tip: Avoid to buy shrimp that have black spots or melanosis on their shell.

Nutritional Information per Serving:

Calories: 310 | **Fat:** 18.9g | **Sat Fat:** 3.7g | **Carbohydrates:** 8.8g | **Fiber:** 4.1g | **Sugar:** 1.5g | **Protein:** 27.3g

4 Weeks Meal Plan

Meal Plan 5 & 1

Week 1

Day 1:

Fueling Hacks:
Hot Chocolate
Brownie Bites
French Toast Sticks
Mac & Cheese Doritos
Blueberry Scones

Lean & Green Meal:
Meatballs & Spinach Soup

Day 2:

Fueling Hacks:
Pumpkin Frappe
Peanut Butter Cups
Potato Bagels
Snickerdoodles
Parmesan Chicken Bites

Lean & Green Meal:
Beef with Carrot & Kale

Day 3:

Fueling Hacks:
Eggnog
Chocolate Cake Fries
Gingersnap Cookies
Sweet Potato Muffins
Chicken Nuggets

Lean & Green Meal:
Chicken & Spinach Stew

Day 4:

Fueling Hacks:
Peppermint Mocha
Brownie Bites
Peanut Butter Cups
Sriracha Popcorn
Gingerbread Biscotti

Lean & Green Meal:
Salmon with Cauliflower Mash

Day 5:

Fueling Hacks:
Berry Mojito
Mini Biscuit Pizza
Peanut Butter Cookies
Gingerbread Biscotti
French Toast Sticks

Lean & Green Meal:
Tofu with Kale

Day 6:

Fueling Hacks:
Coconut Smoothie
Brownie Bites
Mini Biscuit Pizza
Sweet Potato Muffins
French Toast Sticks

Lean & Green Meal:
Ground Beef with Veggies

Day 7:

Fueling Hacks:
Shamrock Shake
Chia Seed Pudding
French Toast Sticks
snicker Doodles
Tortilla Chips

Lean & Green Meal:
Tilapia with Asparagus

Week 2

Day 1:

Fueling Hacks:
Berry Mojito
Peanut Butter Bites
Blueberry Scones
Sweet Potato Muffins
Tortilla Chips

Lean & Green Meal:
Tofu & Mushroom Soup

Day 2:

Fueling Hacks:
Peppermint Mocha
Cheddar Pancakes
Sweet Potato Muffins
Snickerdoodles
Sriracha Popcorn

Lean & Green Meal:
Chicken with Zucchini

Day 3:

Fueling Hacks:
Coconut Smoothie
Mozzarella Pizza Bites
Peanut Butter Cookies
French Toast Sticks
Mac & Cheese Doritos

Lean & Green Meal:
Beef with Broccoli

Day 4:

Fueling Hacks:
Chocolate Frappe
Gingersnap Cookies
Chicken Nuggets
Brownie Bites
Sweet Potato Muffins

Lean & Green Meal:
Turkey Burgers

Day 5:

Fueling Hacks:
Pumpkin Frappe
Gingerbread Biscotti
Mac & Cheese Doritos
Chocolate Cake Fries
Potato Bagels

Lean & Green Meal:
Beef & Cabbage Stew

Day 6:

Fueling Hacks:
Shamrock Shake
Peanut Butter Bites
Potato Bagels
Snickerdoodles
Brownie Bites

Lean & Green Meal:
Shrimp with Spinach

Day 7:

Fueling Hacks:
Pumpkin Frappe
French Toast Sticks
Gingerbread Biscotti
Cheddar Pancakes
Peanut Butter Bites

Lean & Green Meal:
Tofu with Brussels Sprout

Week 3

Day 1:

Fueling Hacks:
Coconut Smoothie
Peanut Butter Bites
Chocolate Cake Fries
Tortilla Chips
Brownie Bites

Lean & Green Meal:
Beef & Bok Choy Soup

Day 2:

Fueling Hacks:
Shamrock Shake
Snickerdoodles
Mozzarella Pizza Bites
Brownie Bites
Blueberry Scones

Lean & Green Meal:
Chicken with Zucchini

Day 3:

Fueling Hacks:
Berry Mojito
Chocolate Cake Fries
Potato Bagels
Gingersnap Cookies
Mac & Cheese Doritos

Lean & Green Meal:
Salmon with Cauliflower Mash

Day 4:

Fueling Hacks:
Pumpkin Spice Latte
Tortilla Chips
Sweet Potato Muffins
French Toast Fries
Sriracha Popcorn

Lean & Green Meal:
Chicken Burgers

Day 5:

Fueling Hacks:
Peppermint Mocha
Peanut Butter Cookies
Parmesan Chicken Bites
Sweet Potato Muffins
Tortilla Chips

Lean & Green Meal:
Beef Chili

Day 6:

Fueling Hacks:
Chocolate Frappe
Peanut Butter Bites
Gingerbread Biscotti
Tortilla Chips
Chocolate Cake Fries

Lean & Green Meal:
Tofu with Kale

Day 7:

Fueling Hacks:
Tiramisu Shake
Gingerbread Biscotti
Snickerdoodles
Cheddar Pancakes
Mini Biscuit Pizza

Lean & Green Meal:
Beef Burgers

Week 4

Day 1:

Fueling Hacks:
Shamrock Shake
Gingersnap Cookies
Chocolate Cake Fries
Tortilla Chips
Parmesan Chicken Bites

Lean & Green Meal:
Beef with Carrot & Kale

Day 2:

Fueling Hacks:
Hot Chocolate
Sriracha Popcorn
Gingerbread Biscotti
Brownie Bites
Cheddar Pancakes

Lean & Green Meal:
Tofu with Brussels Sprout

Day 3:

Fueling Hacks:
Eggnog
Chocolate Cake Fries
Chicken Nuggets
Peanut Butter Cookies
Potato Bagels

Lean & Green Meal:
Turkey with Peas

Day 4:

Fueling Hacks:
Berry Mojito
Snickerdoodles
French Toast Sticks
Brownie Bites
Mini Biscuit Pizza

Lean & Green Meal:
Tilapia with Asparagus

Day 5:

Fueling Hacks:
Chocolate Frappe
Sweet Potato Muffins
Mozzarella Pizza Bites
Peanut Butter Cookies
Sriracha Popcorn

Lean & Green Meal:
Green Chicken Curry

Day 6:

Fueling Hacks:
Peppermint Mocha
Parmesan Chicken Bites
Blueberry Scones
Chocolate Cake Fries
Mac & Cheese Doritos

Lean & Green Meal:
Beef with Bell Peppers

Day 7:

Fueling Hacks:
Coconut Smoothie
Peanut Butter Bites
Gingerbread Biscotti
Potato Bagels
Tortilla Chips

Lean & Green Meal:
Shrimp with Zoodles

Meal Plan 4 & 2 & 1

Week 1

Day 1:

Fueling Hacks:
Berry Mojito
Gingerbread Biscotti
Peanut Butter Cookies
Tortilla Chips

Lean & Green Meals:
Chicken & Zucchini Pancakes
Tofu with Peas

Snack:
½ cup canned peaches (packed in water or natural juices)

Day 2:

Fueling Hacks:
Tiramisu Shake
Chocolate Cake Fries
Sweet Potato Muffins
Sriracha Popcorn

Lean & Green Meals:
Tofu & Mushroom Muffins
Beef Chili

Snack:
¾ cup low-fat plain yogurt

Day 3:

Fueling Hacks:
Chocolate Frappe
Brownie Bites
Blueberry Scones
Mac & Cheese Doritos

Lean & Green Meals:
Chicken with zucchini
Strawberry & Apple Salad

Snack:
1 ounce unsweetened coconut

Day 4:

Fueling Hacks:
Peppermint Mocha
French Toast Sticks
Snickerdoodles
Cheddar Pancakes

Lean & Green Meals:
Beef & Carrot Stew
Salmon Burgers

Snack:
3 celery stalks

Day 5:

Fueling Hacks:
Pumpkin Spice Latte
Peanut Butter Cookies
Sweet Potato Muffins
Mac & Cheese Doritos

Lean & Green Meals:
Green Chicken Curry
Broccoli Frittata

Snack:
½ cup fresh strawberries

Day 6:

Fueling Hacks:
Eggnog
Snickerdoodles

Peanut Butter Cookies
Tortilla Chips

Lean & Green Meals:
Beef & Bok Choy Soup
Tofu with Kale

Snack:
1 cup unsweetened cashew milk

Day 7:

Fueling Hacks:
Pumpkin Frappe
Brownie Bites
Potato Bagels
Snickerdoodles

Lean & Green Meals:
Turkey with Peas
Tofu & Mushroom Soup

Snack:
4 ounces orange

Week 2

Day 1:

Fueling Hacks:
Eggnog
Chicken Nuggets
Snickerdoodles
Sriracha Popcorn

Lean & Green Meals:
Tofu & Mushroom Muffins
chicken & Spinach Stew

Snack:
4 ounces Cherry Tomatoes

Day 2:

Fueling Hacks:
Coconut Smoothie
Mac & Cheese Doritos
French Toast Sticks
Mac & Cheese Doritos

Lean & Green Meals:
Chicken & Veggies Quiche
Shrimp with zoodles

Snack:
4 ounces grapefruit

Day 3:

Fueling Hacks:
Chocolate Frappe
Gingersnap Cookies
Chocolate Cake Fries
Potato Bagels

Lean & Green Meals:
Eggs with Spinach & Tomatoes
Beef & Bok Choy Soup

Snack:
¾ cup low-fat plain yogurt

Day 4:

Fueling Hacks:
Shamrock Shake
Peanut Butter Bites
Chocolate Cake Fries
Tortilla Chips

Lean & Green Meals:
Chicken & Asparagus Frittata
Shrimp with Spinach

Snack:
4 ounces pear

Day 5:

Fueling Hacks:
Shamrock Shake
Mozzarella Pizza Bites

Gingersnap Cookies
Mac & Cheese Doritos

Lean & Green Meals:
Tofu with Kale
Salmon Salad

Snack:
2 hard-boiled eggs

Day 6:

Fueling Hacks:
Pumpkin Spice Latte
Tortilla Chips
Brownie Bites
Blueberry Scones

Lean & Green Meals:
Salmon Burgers
Green Chicken Curry

Snack:
1 ounce unsweetened coconut

Day 7:

Fueling Hacks:
Tiramisu Shake
Gingerbread Biscotti
Mac & Cheese Doritos
Parmesan Chicken Bites

Lean & Green Meals:
Turkey & Zucchini Muffins
Beef with Broccoli

Snack:
½ cup fresh blueberries

Week 3

Day 1:

Fueling Hacks:
Hot Chocolate
Sriracha Popcorn
French Toast Sticks
Brownie Bites

Lean & Green Meals:
Shrimp with Zoodles
Chicken & Orange Salad

Snack:
3 celery stalks

Day 2:

Fueling Hacks:
Peppermint Mocha
Mac & Cheese Doritos
Peanut Butter Cookies
French Toast Sticks

Lean & Green Meals:
Tofu with Broccoli
Ground Beef with Veggies

Snack:
1 cup unsweetened almond milk

Day 3:

Fueling Hacks:
Berry Mojito
Snickerdoodles
Chocolate Cake Fries
Mac & Cheese Doritos

Lean & Green Meals:
Turkey Burgers
Salmon with Cauliflower Mash

Snack:
4 ounces apple

Day 4:

Fueling Hacks:
Coconut Smoothie
Gingerbread Biscotti

Brownie Bites
Mini Biscuit Pizza

Lean & Green Meals:
Strawberry & Asparagus Salad
Beef Chili

Snack:
¾ cup low-fat plain yogurt

Day 5:

Fueling Hacks:
Shamrock Shake
Gingersnap Cookies
Gingerbread Biscotti
Tortilla Chips

Lean & Green Meals:
Green Veggies Quiche
Beef & Cabbage Stew

Snack:
2 hard-boiled eggs

Day 6:

Fueling Hacks:
Peppermint Mocha
Peanut Butter Cookies
French Toast Fries
Sriracha Popcorn

Lean & Green Meals:
Salmon Salad
Meatballs & Spinach Soup

Snack:
½ cup fresh strawberries

Day 7:

Fueling Hacks:
Shamrock Shake
Snickerdoodles
Cheddar Pancakes
Peanut Butter Bites

Lean & Green Meals:
Turkey & Zucchini Muffins
Beef with Bell Peppers

Snack:
½ cup canned peaches (packed in water or natural juices)

Week 4

Day 1:

Fueling Hacks:
Pumpkin Frappe
French Toast Sticks
Potato Bagels
Snickerdoodles

Lean & Green Meals:
Tilapia with Asparagus
Berries & Spinach Salad

Snack:
2 hard-boiled eggs

Day 2:

Fueling Hacks:
Chocolate Frappe
Gingersnap Cookies
Sweet Potato Muffins
Tortilla Chips

Lean & Green Meals:
Beef Burgers
Turkey with Peas

Snack:
15-20 black olives

Day 3:

Fueling Hacks:
Coconut Smoothie
Brownie Bites

Peanut Butter Cookies
French Toast Sticks

Lean & Green Meals:
Chicken & Orange Salad
Tofu with Kale

Snack:
1 cup unsweetened cashew milk

Day 4:

Fueling Hacks:
Shamrock Shake
Peanut Butter Cookies
French Toast Sticks
Chicken Nuggets

Lean & Green Meals:
Chicken & Asparagus Frittata
Beef Chili

Snack:
3 celery stalks

Day 5:

Fueling Hacks:
Chocolate Frappe
Gingersnap Cookies
Potato Bagels
Snickerdoodles

Lean & Green Meals:
Kale & Mushroom Muffins
Beef & Bok Choy Soup

Snack:
4 ounces plums

Day 6:

Fueling Hacks:
Shamrock Shake
Snickerdoodles
Gingersnap Cookies
Mac & Cheese Doritos

Lean & Green Meals:
Chicken & Zucchini Pancakes
Salmon with Cauliflower Mash

Snack:
15-20 black olives

Day 7:

Fueling Hacks:
Berry Mojito
Chocolate Cake Fries
Gingersnap Cookies
Mac & Cheese Doritos

Lean & Green Meals:
Chicken Burgers
Beef with Bell Peppers

Snack:
½ cup canned pears (packed in water or natural juices)

Conclusion

The Lean & Green Diet is primarily based on having lean & green meals with consuming small portions throughout the day along with special fuelings. The diet promotes strategic and healthy weight loss, which is very easy to achieve by simply following the diet. There are two prominent plans in the Lean & Green Diet, i.e., the 5 & 1 plan and the 4 & 2 & 1 plan. The prior is considered optimal for those people who want to achieve a very drastic and rapid weight loss by only consuming 800 calories per day. Whereas the latter is for those people who want to have a relatively slower weight loss or if they want to maintain their current weight. The Lean & Green Diet utmost convenience, clarity in food choices, and rapid weight loss to its followers.

Copyright © 2021

All Right Reserved.

Under no circumstances, no part of this publication may be reproduced, distributed, or transmitted in any form or by any means, including photocopying, recording, or other electronic or mechanical methods, or by any information storage and retrieval system without the prior written permission of the copyright holder.

The information in this book is accurate and complete, however, the author and the publisher do not warrant the accuracy of the information, text and graphics contained within the book due to the rapidly changing nature of science, research, known and unknown facts and internet. The author and the publisher do not hold any responsibility for errors, omissions or contrary interpretation of the subject matter herein. This book is presented solely for motivational and informational purposes only.

www.ingramcontent.com/pod-product-compliance
Lightning Source LLC
Chambersburg PA
CBHW080608170426
43209CB00007B/1368